5-INGREDIENTS High-Protein Dishes

GARDEN of GRAPES.

First Edition: 2023

Published by Garden of Grapes.

Printed in USA

The recipes, techniques, and tips in this cookbook are intended for personal use only. The author and publisher are not responsible for any adverse effects or consequences resulting from the use of the recipes or suggestions in this book.

Library of Congress Cataloging-in-Publication Data:

First edition.
Includes index.

Manufactured in USA

Introduction

Ladies and gentlemen, fellow culinary explorers,

Allow me to extend a heartfelt welcome to the gastronomic journey that awaits you within the pages of "5-Ingredient High-Protein Dishes." As we embark on this adventure, I want to give you a taste of what you'll discover in the following chapters and why this particular cookbook came to be.

In the ever-evolving world of culinary delights, one thing remains constant: the quest for simplicity and flavor. It's a pursuit that has inspired chefs throughout history, from the grand kitchens of Europe to the bustling street food stalls of Southeast Asia. It's this very quest that breathes life into our 5-ingredient culinary creations.

The concept of simplicity isn't new, but it is timeless. From the humblest kitchen to the most prestigious restaurant, there's a common thread - the desire for meals that are uncomplicated yet extraordinarily delicious. The fusion of minimalism and bold, unforgettable flavors is the essence of our book.

So, why "5-Ingredient High-Protein Dishes"? In today's fast-paced world, time and simplicity are precious commodities. We've all been there - those moments when you want a satisfying, protein-packed meal without spending hours in the kitchen. This book was born from the idea that you can whip up a hearty, protein-rich dish with just a handful of ingredients and a dash of inspiration.

As I stand before my stove, I often ponder the importance of a good meal. It's not just about sustenance; it's about the joy of creation, the satisfaction of taste, and the connections it forges. Food, in all its simplicity and complexity, is a universal language that speaks to the soul.

Inside this cookbook, you'll find an array of high-protein dishes that tantalize the taste buds and provide the nourishment you seek. From succulent poultry to savory plant-based options, each recipe has been meticulously crafted to ensure your culinary experience is nothing short of extraordinary.

You can expect a curated selection of recipes that are easy to follow and quick to prepare. We've sifted through the vast realm of culinary possibilities to bring you only the best. Whether you're a seasoned chef or a novice in the kitchen, there's something here for everyone. The recipes are designed to streamline the cooking process, allowing you to focus on the joys of food rather than the complexities of the kitchen.

With "5-Ingredient High-Protein Dishes," my goal is to inspire you to create mouthwatering meals effortlessly. So, get ready to embark on a journey that celebrates the art of simplicity and the mastery of flavor. It's a culinary adventure where taste knows no bounds, and every dish is a testament to the beauty of keeping it deliciously simple.

Let's dive into this world of flavor together, and may your kitchen be forever filled with delightful high-protein creations.

Cooking Philosophy or Approach

Cooking Philosophy:

In the world of culinary creativity, there exists a beautiful paradox. It's the dance of simplicity and artistry, where a handful of carefully selected ingredients can create symphonies of flavor. This cookbook, "5-Ingredient High-Protein Dishes," embodies that philosophy. We believe that great food doesn't have to be complicated; it should be accessible, nutritious, and above all, delicious.

Our Approach to Food:

Here, we embrace the minimalist approach to cooking. It's about letting the ingredients speak for themselves, allowing their natural flavors and textures to shine. High-protein dishes, often seen as complex or reserved for the pros, can be approachable for every home chef. Our mission is to demystify high-protein cooking, showing that it can be both straightforward and palate-pleasing.

Simplicity and Innovation:

Our recipes in this cookbook are a harmonious blend of tradition and innovation. We respect the foundations of classic cooking while weaving in modern ideas. From familiar favorites like succulent roast chicken to exciting new creations such as quinoa-stuffed bell peppers, each dish exemplifies our core philosophy—simple, accessible, and nutritious.

Ingredient Selection:

The selection of ingredients is paramount in our culinary journey. We focus on ingredients that provide high-quality protein. You'll find lean meats, plant-based proteins, and seafood that not only tantalize your taste buds but also nourish your body. The star of each recipe, the protein source, is celebrated and treated with respect.

Techniques:

Technique is the heartbeat of our cookbook. We emphasize fundamental cooking methods that ensure your dishes turn out perfectly every time. Searing, grilling, roasting, and sautéing are techniques we cherish. These methods, when applied with care, transform basic ingredients into extraordinary creations.

Flavor Profiles:

Flavor reigns supreme in our kitchen. Our recipes encompass a diverse range of flavors, from the comforting richness of slow-cooked stews to the zesty vibrancy of grilled skewers. We believe that the complexity of flavors can be achieved without complexity in preparation.

Adventurous Spirit:

Cooking is an adventure, a journey into the heart of your kitchen. In this cookbook, you'll find room for experimentation. We encourage you to adapt and modify these recipes to suit your personal taste, dietary requirements, or culinary curiosity. Each dish is a canvas, and you are the artist.

Inclusivity:

While this cookbook focuses on high-protein dishes, it also respects dietary diversity. You'll find options for various dietary preferences, ensuring that everyone can partake in the joy of exceptional food.

Pictures Included:

For us, a picture is not just a visual accompaniment. It's a way to ignite your culinary imagination, to make your taste buds tingle before you even step into the kitchen. The pictures included are more than just a guide; they're an invitation to embark on a sensory journey.

In conclusion, our culinary philosophy revolves around the idea that five ingredients, when chosen wisely and prepared with heart, can create meals that bring joy, nourishment, and a touch of elegance to your table. We invite you to join us in celebrating the art of high-protein simplicity, and in the words of the great Julia Child, "The only real stumbling block is fear of failure. In cooking, you've got to have a what-the-hell attitude." Embrace the journey, and may your kitchen be filled with delightful high-protein dishes.

With culinary passion,
Garden of Grapes

Tips for Successful Cooking

Listen up, you intrepid home chefs and culinary explorers, for I have some wisdom to impart. As you embark on your journey through the gastronomic wonderland of "5-Ingredient High-Protein Dishes," it's important to be armed with a few kitchen tips and techniques. These nuggets of culinary guidance will ensure that your cooking adventures are as smooth as a perfectly whipped meringue.

1. Preparation is Key: Before you even think about turning on the stove, get all your ingredients in order. This means chopping, dicing, and measuring everything you need. Mise en place, as the pros say. It saves time and prevents frantic searches for that elusive spice while something's sizzling away.

2. Quality Matters: When it comes to ingredients, quality reigns supreme. Fresh produce, top-notch proteins, and aromatic spices can elevate a simple dish to a gourmet masterpiece. Don't be afraid to splurge a bit on the essentials; your taste buds will thank you.

3. Balancing Flavors: A well-balanced dish is a symphony of flavors. It's not just about spicing things up; it's about achieving harmony. Taste as you go, and adjust the seasoning as needed. A pinch of salt, a dash of acid, or a sprinkle of sweet can make all the difference.

4. Cooking Temperatures: Different ingredients require different cooking temperatures. Searing a steak? High heat is your friend. Simmering a delicate sauce? Low and slow is the way to go. Understanding these nuances will prevent overcooking and ensure your meals are cooked to perfection.

5. Resting Time: Let your creations rest. When you remove a sizzling steak from the heat or pull a golden loaf of bread from the oven, don't rush to dig in. Allow them to rest, so the juices redistribute, and the flavors meld. Your patience will be rewarded.

6. Clean as You Go: A cluttered, messy kitchen is a recipe for chaos. Take a page from the pros and clean as you go. It makes the entire cooking process smoother and less daunting.

7. Experiment and Have Fun: Cooking is an art, not an exact science. Don't be afraid to get creative and experiment with flavors and techniques. Some of the most delicious discoveries happen by accident.

In this culinary adventure, ingredient selection is paramount. Opt for the freshest, highest quality ingredients you can get your hands on. Whether it's a succulent cut of meat, a vibrant bundle of herbs, or the ripest vegetables, each element contributes to the overall excellence of your dish.

So, as you dive into the recipes of "5-Ingredient High-Protein Dishes," remember these tips. Let your kitchen be your canvas, and your cooking, a masterpiece. Whether you're a seasoned home cook or just starting your culinary journey, these insights will serve you well. Now, onwards to delicious, high-protein creations!

Kitchen Essentials

Alright, my fellow kitchen warriors, before we dive into the culinary battleground that is "5-Ingredient High-Protein Dishes," let's make sure we've got our arsenal of kitchen tools and equipment lined up. Remember, the right tools can turn an ordinary meal into a culinary masterpiece.

Kitchen Essentials:

1. Chef's Knife: This trusty companion is your ultimate kitchen sidekick. Invest in a high-quality, sharp chef's knife – it's worth every penny.

2. Cutting Board: A sturdy cutting board provides a safe platform for all your chopping and slicing endeavors.

3. Non-Stick Skillet: Perfect for those high-protein sears and sautés without the sticky aftermath.

4. Saucepan: A versatile piece of kitchen equipment. Great for simmering sauces and cooking grains.

5. Baking Sheet: From roasted vegetables to protein-packed sheet pan dinners, this is your go-to.

6. Blender: For those protein-packed smoothies and sauces, a quality blender is essential.

7. Measuring Cups and Spoons: Precision matters, especially in baking. So, make sure you've got these on hand.

8. Mixing Bowls: Get yourself an assortment of sizes, and you're ready to tackle anything from salads to baking projects.

9. Whisk: Whip, blend, and stir your way to success with this kitchen essential.

10. Tongs: These long-armed utensils are ideal for turning food without getting too close to the heat.

Tips for Using Your Kitchen Arsenal Effectively:

1. Keep Your Knives Sharp: A dull knife is a dangerous one. Regularly sharpen your chef's knife to make your chopping and slicing a breeze.

2. Master the Art of Temperature: Learn to control the heat. Your skillet should sizzle when you add ingredients, but you don't want to incinerate them.

3. Preheat Your Pans: Whether you're using a skillet or saucepan, preheating ensures even cooking.

4. Read Recipes Twice: Before you start, give the recipe a good read-through. This helps you understand the steps and prep work involved.

5. Mise en Place: This fancy French term simply means "everything in its place." Before you start cooking, measure and prep all your ingredients. It makes the process smoother.

6. Taste as You Go: Don't hesitate to taste your creation as you cook. It's the chef's prerogative!

7. Keep it Clean: Clean as you go. Trust me, it makes the whole process less daunting.

8. Experiment: High-protein cooking is all about creativity. Feel free to tweak recipes to your taste.

Now that you're armed with the right gear and tips, let's venture into the world of high-protein culinary wizardry. With your kitchen essentials and newfound skills, there's no recipe you can't conquer.

Onward, my fellow epicurean warriors! The battle for delicious high-protein dishes awaits, and victory is just a few ingredients away.

Flavor Pairing Suggestions

So, you've ventured into the world of 5-Ingredient High-Protein Dishes, and you're yearning to take your culinary creativity up a notch. I get it; the call of the kitchen can be irresistible. You've mastered the art of simplicity, and now, it's time to explore the endless possibilities of flavor pairings.

Here's where the real fun begins. Think of this as your culinary playground, a place to experiment, create, and craft your own culinary masterpieces. The essence of great cooking lies not only in the ingredients you choose but in how you balance and pair their flavors.

1. Sweet and Savory
Ever tried the sweet-savory combo? Think about the rich, umami taste of soy sauce mingling with the sweet kiss of honey. Or the delightful marriage of juicy chicken with a sticky, sweet barbecue sauce. These are contrasts that create magic on your taste buds. Try it with your high-protein creations. A drizzle of honey on your roasted chicken, a sprinkle of sea salt on your chocolatey protein pancakes – it's a world of endless possibilities.

2. Fresh and Zesty
A touch of freshness can breathe life into your dishes. Imagine the zest of a lemon awakening the flavors of a simple grilled fish. The same applies to your high-protein meals. Fresh herbs like basil, cilantro, or mint can turn an ordinary dish into a vibrant, zesty sensation. A handful of fresh arugula or microgreens can lend a peppery crunch to your high-protein salads. Don't shy away from the zest; it's the secret to elevating your dishes.

3. Creamy and Tangy
Creamy textures meet tangy flavors – it's a match made in culinary heaven. Take your creamy mashed potatoes and add a dollop of tangy Greek yogurt. The result? A velvety, tangy dream. For your high-protein dishes, experiment with Greek yogurt-based sauces, tzatziki, or a zingy lemon tahini dressing. The creaminess balances perfectly with the tang, creating harmonious bites every time.

4. Nutty and Earthy
Nuts, seeds, and earthy ingredients can add depth to your dishes. Picture a sprinkle of toasted almonds on your protein-rich quinoa salad, or a dash of sesame seeds on your seared tofu. The nutty, earthy notes complement the high-protein foundation, creating a complex and satisfying experience.

5. Spicy and Cooling
Spice enthusiasts, this one's for you. Balance the heat of your favorite chili flakes or hot sauce with cooling elements. A dash of yogurt can cool down a fiery curry, and a cucumber-mint salsa can accompany your spicy grilled meats. The interplay of spice and coolness not only tantalizes your palate but keeps you coming back for more.

The beauty of these flavor pairings lies in their versatility. Don't hesitate to mix and match, to experiment and improvise. The culinary world is your canvas, and you are the artist. Your 5-Ingredient High-Protein Dishes are the perfect backdrop for your flavorful creations.

So, go ahead, step into your culinary playground, and let your imagination run wild. With these flavor pairing suggestions, you're equipped to craft dishes that are uniquely yours. Your taste buds will thank you for the adventure.

Remember, there are no rules in this playground – only flavors, endless inspiration, and delicious surprises.

Happy pairing!

- Garden of Grapes

Table of contents

Chapter 1: Lean Meat Marvels

4 servings | 190 cal | 15 mins

Grilled Chicken Breast

A classic that never goes out of style! This recipe originated in the Mediterranean and has been loved for generations.

Ingredients:

4 boneless chicken breasts (6 oz each)
2 tbsp olive oil
1 tsp salt
1/2 tsp black pepper
1/2 tsp paprika
1/2 tsp garlic powder
1/2 tsp onion powder

Directions

1. Preheat the grill to medium-high heat.
2. Brush chicken with olive oil and season with spices.
3. Grill for 6-7 mins per side until cooked through.

Serve hot.

Fun Facts

Chicken is an excellent source of lean protein, perfect for a post-workout meal.

2 servings

330 cal

20 mins

Baked Salmon

This salmon dish hails from the Nordic seas. Its rich, buttery flavor is complemented by a zesty lemon drizzle.

Ingredients:

2 salmon fillets (6 oz each)
2 tbsp melted butter
1 lemon, sliced
2 cloves garlic, minced
Salt and pepper to taste

Directions

1. Preheat oven to 375°F (190°C).
2. Place salmon on a baking sheet.
3. Drizzle with butter, add lemon and garlic, and season.
4. Bake for 15 mins. Serve with love.

Fun Facts

Salmon is packed with omega-3 fatty acids, promoting heart health and brain function.

4 servings | 280 cal | 10 mins

Turkey and Avocado Wraps

An American favorite! These wraps are perfect for a quick lunch. The combination of turkey and avocado is heavenly.

Ingredients:

4 whole wheat tortillas
8 oz turkey slices
1 ripe avocado, sliced
1/2 cup lettuce, shredded
1/4 cup mayonnaise

Directions

1. Lay out tortillas and spread mayonnaise on each.
2. Layer turkey, avocado, and lettuce.
3. Roll tightly, slice, and enjoy!

Fun Facts

Avocado is known as "butter fruit" due to its creamy texture and healthy fats.

4
servings

220 cal

12 mins

Lemon Garlic Shrimp

This zesty shrimp dish has its roots in the coastal regions of Italy. Its vibrant flavors will transport you to the seaside.

Ingredients:

1 lb large shrimp, peeled and deveined
2 tbsp olive oil
4 cloves garlic, minced
Juice of 1 lemon
Zest of 1 lemon
Salt and pepper

Directions

1. Heat olive oil in a pan over medium heat.
2. Sauté garlic until fragrant.
3. Add shrimp, cook until pink.
4. Add lemon juice, zest, salt, and pepper.
Serve with pasta.

Fun Facts

Shrimp is a low-calorie, high-protein option, perfect for a guilt-free indulgence.

2 servings

240 cal

15 mins

Seared Tuna Steaks

This Japanese-inspired recipe is a culinary masterpiece. The seared tuna steaks are a delight for both the eyes and the palate.

Ingredients:

2 tuna steaks (6 oz each)
2 tbsp sesame oil
1 tbsp soy sauce
1 tsp sesame seeds
Salt and pepper to taste

Directions

1. Season tuna with salt and pepper.
2. Heat sesame oil in a pan over high heat.
3. Sear tuna for 1-2 mins per side.
4. Drizzle with soy sauce and sprinkle sesame seeds. Serve promptly.

Fun Facts

Tuna is a powerhouse of vitamins and minerals, enhancing your overall health.

4 servings

320 cal

20 mins

Beef and Broccoli Stir-Fry

A taste of Chinese cuisine at home! The savory beef pairs perfectly with tender broccoli in this flavorful stir-fry.

Ingredients:

1 lb flank steak, thinly sliced
2 cups broccoli florets
1/4 cup soy sauce
2 tbsp honey
2 cloves garlic, minced
1 tsp ginger, minced
1 tsp cornstarch

Directions

1. In a bowl, mix soy sauce, honey, garlic, ginger, and cornstarch.
2. Heat a wok, stir-fry beef until brown.
3. Add broccoli and sauce, cook until thickened. Serve over rice.

Fun Facts

Broccoli is rich in vitamins, especially vitamin C, which boosts your immune system.

4 servings | 260 cal | 25 mins

Pork Tenderloin with Dijon Glaze

Easy

French-inspired and utterly delicious! The Dijon glaze adds a tangy twist to this succulent pork tenderloin.

Ingredients:

1 lb pork tenderloin
2 tbsp Dijon mustard
2 tbsp honey
2 cloves garlic, minced
1 tsp thyme
Salt and pepper to taste

Directions

1. Preheat oven to 375°F (190°C).
2. Mix Dijon, honey, garlic, thyme, salt, and pepper.
3. Rub mixture on pork.
4. Roast for 20-25 mins until cooked. Slice and serve.

Fun Facts

Dijon mustard originated in Dijon, France, and is celebrated for its distinctive flavor.

4 servings | 280 cal | 20 mins

Garlic Butter Steak Bites

A delectable appetizer that's perfect for sharing! These steak bites with garlic butter are a crowd-pleaser at any gathering.

Ingredients:

1 lb sirloin steak, cut into bite-sized pieces
2 tbsp butter
4 cloves garlic, minced
1 tsp fresh parsley, chopped
Salt and pepper to taste

Directions

1. Season steak with salt and pepper.
2. Heat a skillet, melt butter, add garlic.
3. Sear steak until desired doneness.
4. Garnish with parsley. Serve hot.

Fun Facts

Garlic is not only flavorful but also has numerous health benefits, including immune support.

4 servings | 220 cal | 30 mins

Herb-Roasted Turkey Breast

A Thanksgiving favorite that can be enjoyed year-round. The herb-infused turkey breast is succulent and full of flavor.

Ingredients:

1 turkey breast (2 lbs)
2 tbsp olive oil
2 tsp rosemary, chopped
2 tsp thyme, chopped
2 tsp sage, chopped
Salt and pepper to taste

Directions

1. Preheat oven to 350°F (175°C).
2. Mix olive oil, herbs, salt, and pepper.
3. Rub mixture over the turkey.
4. Roast for 25-30 mins, until the internal temp reaches 165°F. Slice and serve.

Fun Facts

Turkey is a lean meat that's rich in protein and a great source of vitamins and minerals.

2 servings

360 cal

25 mins

Rosemary Lamb Chops

A touch of elegance on your plate! These rosemary-infused lamb chops are tender and flavorful, making any meal special.

Ingredients:

4 lamb chops (4 oz each)
2 tbsp olive oil
2 cloves garlic, minced
1 tsp rosemary, minced
Salt and pepper to taste

Directions

1. Season lamb chops with salt, pepper, and rosemary.
2. Heat olive oil in a pan.
3. Sear chops for 3-4 mins per side.
Serve with your favorite side dishes.

Fun Facts

Lamb is a rich source of high-quality protein and essential nutrients for overall health.

Chapter 2: Vegetarian Protein Power

4 servings | 320 cal | 30 mins

Chickpea Curry

A vibrant and comforting dish with roots in Indian cuisine. This chickpea curry is a vegetarian delight.

Ingredients:

2 cans (15 oz each) chickpeas, drained
1 onion, chopped
2 cloves garlic, minced
1 can (14 oz) diced tomatoes
2 tbsp curry powder
1/2 cup coconut milk
Salt and pepper to taste

Directions

1. In a pan, sauté onions and garlic until fragrant.
2. Add chickpeas, tomatoes, and curry powder.
3. Simmer for 20 mins.
4. Stir in coconut milk. Serve over rice.

Fun Facts

Chickpeas are high in fiber and protein, making this curry a nutritious and satisfying meal.

4 servings · 250 cal · 25 mins

Tofu Stir-Fry

An Asian-inspired stir-fry that's quick and packed with protein. Tofu, vegetables, and a savory sauce.

Ingredients:

1 package (14 oz) extra-firm tofu, cubed
2 cups mixed vegetables
2 tbsp soy sauce
1 tbsp sesame oil
2 cloves garlic, minced
1 tsp ginger, minced
Salt and pepper

Directions

1. Heat sesame oil in a wok, add garlic and ginger.
2. Stir-fry tofu until golden.
3. Add vegetables, soy sauce, salt, and pepper.
4. Cook until veggies are tender. Serve with rice.

Fun Facts

Tofu is an excellent source of plant-based protein, and it takes on the flavors of the stir-fry beautifully.

4 servings | 280 cal | 20 mins

Quinoa Salad with Black Beans

A refreshing and filling salad that combines protein-packed quinoa with black beans and a zesty dressing.

Ingredients:

1 cup quinoa
1 can (15 oz) black beans, drained
1 cup corn kernels
1 red bell pepper, diced
1/4 cup cilantro, chopped
2 tbsp olive oil
2 tbsp lime juice
Salt and pepper

Directions

1. Cook quinoa according to package instructions.
2. In a bowl, combine quinoa, black beans, corn, pepper, and cilantro.
3. Whisk together olive oil, lime juice, salt, and pepper. Drizzle over the salad.

Fun Facts

Quinoa is a complete protein, providing all essential amino acids, making this salad a nutritional powerhouse.

4 servings | 220 cal | 40 mins

Lentil Soup

This hearty lentil soup is a classic, brimming with protein and comforting flavors.

Ingredients:

1 cup brown or green lentils
1 onion, chopped
2 carrots, diced
2 celery stalks, diced
2 cloves garlic, minced
1 tsp cumin
1 tsp paprika
6 cups vegetable broth
Salt and pepper

Directions

1. In a pot, sauté onions, carrots, celery, and garlic until soft.
2. Add lentils, cumin, paprika, and broth.
3. Simmer for 30 mins.
4. Season with salt and pepper. Serve hot.

Fun Facts

Lentils are rich in protein, fiber, and various essential nutrients, promoting a healthy diet.

4 servings | 180 cal | 30 mins

Spinach and Feta Stuffed Portobello Mushrooms

These stuffed mushrooms are a delightful combination of earthy Portobellos, spinach, and creamy feta cheese.

Ingredients:

4 large Portobello mushrooms
2 cups fresh spinach, chopped
1/2 cup feta cheese, crumbled
2 cloves garlic, minced
2 tbsp olive oil
Salt and pepper to taste

Directions

1. Remove mushroom stems, brush caps with olive oil, and season with salt and pepper.
2. In a pan, sauté spinach and garlic until wilted.
3. Fill mushrooms with the spinach and feta mixture.
4. Bake at 375°F (190°C) for 20 mins.

Fun Facts

Portobello mushrooms are low in calories and rich in antioxidants, making them a healthy choice.

4 servings | 260 cal | 35 mins

Tempeh and Vegetable Skewers

These skewers combine marinated tempeh and colorful vegetables for a tasty, protein-packed barbecue treat.

Ingredients:

1 package (8 oz) tempeh, cubed
2 bell peppers, diced
1 zucchini, sliced
1 red onion, diced
For marinade: 2 tbsp soy sauce
2 tbsp balsamic vinegar
2 cloves garlic, minced
2 tbsp olive oil
Salt and pepper

Directions

1. In a bowl, whisk together marinade ingredients.
2. Thread tempeh and veggies onto skewers.
3. Grill or broil until charred and cooked, brushing with marinade. Serve with rice or salad.

Fun Facts

Tempeh is a fermented soy product high in protein and probiotics, benefiting gut health.

4 servings

230 cal

15 mins

Edamame Salad

A simple and refreshing salad featuring edamame, which adds a protein punch.

Ingredients:

2 cups shelled edamame
1 cucumber, diced
1 red onion, finely chopped
1/4 cup fresh mint, chopped
2 tbsp rice vinegar
2 tbsp sesame oil
Salt and pepper to taste

Directions

1. Cook edamame according to package instructions, then cool.
2. In a bowl, combine edamame, cucumber, onion, and mint.
3. Whisk together rice vinegar, sesame oil, salt, and pepper. Drizzle over the salad.

Fun Facts

Edamame is young soybeans and a great source of plant-based protein, making this salad both nutritious and delicious.

4 servings | 300 cal | 25 mins

Easy

Black Bean Quesadillas

These quesadillas are filled with black beans, cheese, and spices, creating a satisfying and protein-rich meal.

Ingredients:

4 large flour tortillas
1 can (15 oz) black beans, drained and mashed
1 cup cheddar cheese, shredded
1/2 cup corn kernels
1/4 cup cilantro, chopped
1 tsp chili powder
Salt and pepper

Directions

1. Spread black beans on half of each tortilla.
2. Sprinkle cheese, corn, cilantro, chili powder, salt, and pepper.
3. Fold tortillas in half.
4. Heat in a pan until golden on both sides. Slice and serve.

Fun Facts

Black beans are a great source of plant-based protein and fiber, promoting fullness and digestive health.

4 servings | 180 cal | 10 mins

Super Easy

Greek Yogurt Parfait

A quick and healthy dessert or breakfast option. Layers of Greek yogurt, berries, and granola for added crunch.

Ingredients:

2 cups Greek yogurt
1 cup mixed berries (strawberries, blueberries, raspberries)
1/2 cup granola
2 tbsp honey
A pinch of cinnamon and nutmeg

Directions

1. In serving glasses, layer Greek yogurt, berries, granola, and honey.
2. Sprinkle with cinnamon and nutmeg.
3. Repeat for multiple layers. Serve chilled.

Fun Facts

Greek yogurt is high in protein and probiotics, beneficial for gut health and overall wellness.

4 servings | 250 cal | 20 mins

Spinach and Lentil Salad

A refreshing salad with a blend of hearty lentils, fresh spinach, and a zesty lemon vinaigrette.

Ingredients:

1 cup brown or green lentils
4 cups fresh spinach
1/4 cup red onion, thinly sliced
1/4 cup feta cheese, crumbled
2 tbsp olive oil
2 tbsp lemon juice
1 tsp Dijon mustard
Salt and pepper

Directions

1. Cook lentils according to package instructions, then cool.
2. In a bowl, combine lentils, spinach, red onion, and feta cheese.
3. Whisk together olive oil, lemon juice, Dijon mustard, salt, and pepper. Drizzle over the salad.

Fun Facts

Lentils are rich in protein, fiber, and various vitamins and minerals, promoting a balanced diet.

Chapter 3: Eggs for Every Meal

2 servings | 220 cal | 15 mins

Scrambled Eggs with Spinach

These scrambled eggs with a twist of spinach are a nutritious way to start the day.

Ingredients:

4 large eggs
1 cup fresh spinach, chopped
2 tbsp butter
Salt and pepper to taste

Directions

1. In a bowl, whisk eggs and season with salt and pepper.
2. In a pan, melt butter and sauté spinach until wilted.
3. Pour in eggs and scramble until cooked to your liking. Serve hot.

Fun Facts

Spinach is rich in iron and vitamins, making this dish a healthy and delicious breakfast choice.

2 servings

290 cal

20 mins

Poached Eggs with Avocado

A simple but satisfying dish featuring perfectly poached eggs served on a bed of creamy avocado.

Ingredients:

2 large eggs
1 ripe avocado, sliced
2 slices of whole-grain bread
1 tsp white vinegar
Salt and pepper to taste

Directions

1. Toast bread slices.
2. In a pan, bring water to a simmer with vinegar.
3. Gently crack eggs into the simmering water and poach for 4-5 mins.
4. Serve poached eggs on avocado slices, season with salt and pepper. Serve with toasted bread.

Fun Facts

Avocado is packed with healthy fats and provides a creamy texture, enhancing the dish's flavor.

4 servings | 200 cal | 20 mins

Egg Salad

A classic egg salad recipe, perfect for sandwiches or as a topping for a refreshing salad.

Ingredients:

6 large hard-boiled eggs, chopped
1/4 cup mayonnaise
1/4 cup plain Greek yogurt
2 tsp Dijon mustard
2 green onions, sliced
1 tsp paprika
Salt and pepper to taste

Directions

1. In a bowl, combine chopped eggs, mayonnaise, Greek yogurt, Dijon mustard, green onions, paprika, salt, and pepper.
2. Mix well and refrigerate for at least 30 mins. Serve as a sandwich filling or on a bed of greens.

Fun Facts

Eggs are a great source of protein, and this salad adds creaminess and flavor to your meals.

2 servings

280 cal

20 mins

Omelette with Mushrooms and Cheese

A cheesy and savory omelette filled with sautéed mushrooms. Perfect for breakfast or brunch.

Ingredients:

4 large eggs
1 cup mushrooms, sliced
1/2 cup cheddar cheese, grated
2 tbsp butter
Salt and pepper to taste

Directions

1. In a bowl, whisk eggs and season with salt and pepper.
2. In a non-stick pan, melt butter and sauté mushrooms until tender.
3. Pour in whisked eggs and cook until set.
4. Sprinkle cheese over one half of the omelette and fold it. Serve hot.

Fun Facts

Mushrooms provide a meaty texture, and cheese adds richness to this classic omelette.

8 servings | 140 cal | 25 mins

Easy

Deviled Eggs

A timeless appetizer with a zesty twist. Deviled eggs are a hit at gatherings and parties.

Ingredients:

4 hard-boiled eggs, cut in half
2 tbsp mayonnaise
1 tsp Dijon mustard
1 tsp pickle relish
Paprika and chives for garnish
Salt and pepper to taste

Directions

1. Remove yolks from egg halves and place them in a bowl.
2. Mix yolks with mayonnaise, Dijon mustard, pickle relish, salt, and pepper.
3. Fill egg whites with the yolk mixture.
4. Garnish with paprika and chives. Serve chilled.

Fun Facts

Deviled eggs are a classic party favorite, and the variations are endless for added flair.

4
servings

330 cal

30 mins

Shakshuka

A Middle Eastern delight! Shakshuka is a flavorful dish of poached eggs in a spiced tomato and pepper sauce.

Ingredients:

4 large eggs
1 can (14 oz) diced tomatoes
1 red bell pepper, chopped
1 onion, chopped
2 cloves garlic, minced
2 tsp cumin
2 tsp paprika
Salt and pepper to taste

Directions

1. In a skillet, sauté onions, peppers, and garlic until soft.
2. Add tomatoes and spices, simmer for 15 mins.
3. Make small wells in the sauce and crack eggs into them.
4. Cover and cook until eggs are set. Serve with crusty bread.

Fun Facts

Shakshuka is not only delicious but also provides a hearty and satisfying meal for any time of day.

2 servings | 250 cal | 15 mins

Egg and Spinach Breakfast Wrap

A nutritious and portable breakfast option. Scrambled eggs, spinach, and cheese wrapped in a tortilla.

Ingredients:

4 large eggs
2 cups fresh spinach, chopped
1/2 cup cheddar cheese, grated
2 large whole-wheat tortillas
Salt and pepper to taste

Directions

1. In a bowl, whisk eggs and season with salt and pepper.
2. Scramble eggs and spinach in a pan until cooked.
3. Divide the egg mixture between tortillas and sprinkle with cheese.
4. Roll up the tortillas and serve.

Fun Facts

This breakfast wrap is a great on-the-go option, combining protein, veggies, and cheesy goodness.

4 servings

300 cal

30 mins

Asparagus and Goat Cheese Frittata

A delightful frittata with asparagus spears and creamy goat cheese, perfect for brunch or a light dinner.

Ingredients:

8 large eggs
1 bunch asparagus, trimmed and cut into 1-inch pieces
1/2 cup crumbled goat cheese
2 tbsp olive oil
Salt and pepper to taste

Directions

1. Preheat oven to 350°F (175°C).
2. In an oven-safe skillet, sauté asparagus in olive oil until tender.
3. Whisk eggs, salt, and pepper, and pour over the asparagus.
4. Sprinkle goat cheese on top.
5. Bake for 20-25 mins until set. Serve hot.

Fun Facts

Asparagus adds a fresh crunch, and goat cheese provides a creamy contrast in this frittata.

4 servings | 360 cal | 25 mins

Egg and Bacon Breakfast Tacos

Breakfast tacos with a savory twist! Scrambled eggs, crispy bacon, and fresh salsa all wrapped in soft tortillas.

Ingredients:

8 large eggs
8 slices bacon, cooked and crumbled
8 small flour tortillas
1 cup salsa
Salt and pepper to taste

Directions

1. In a bowl, whisk eggs, season with salt and pepper, and scramble in a pan.
2. Warm tortillas in a dry skillet.
3. Fill each tortilla with eggs, bacon, and salsa.
4. Roll up and serve hot.

Fun Facts

Bacon adds a smoky flavor and a crispy texture to these breakfast tacos, a savory morning treat.

4 servings | 400 cal | 30 mins

Eggs Benedict

A classic brunch dish that combines poached eggs, Canadian bacon, and creamy hollandaise sauce on English muffins.

Ingredients:

4 large eggs
4 English muffins, split
8 slices Canadian bacon
For hollandaise sauce: 4 large egg yolks
1 tsp lemon juice
1/2 cup unsalted butter
Cayenne pepper, salt, and pepper to taste

Directions

1. In a double boiler, whisk egg yolks and lemon juice until thick.
2. Gradually whisk in melted butter.
3. Season with cayenne pepper, salt, and pepper.
4. Toast English muffins, top each half with Canadian bacon, a poached egg, and hollandaise sauce. Serve hot.

Fun Facts

Eggs Benedict is a rich and indulgent brunch favorite that's worth the effort for a special occasion.

Chapter 4: Protein-Packed Pasta

4 servings | 420 cal | 30 mins

Chicken Alfredo

A creamy and indulgent classic! This chicken Alfredo pasta is the ultimate comfort food.

Ingredients:

8 oz fettuccine pasta
2 boneless, skinless chicken breasts (8 oz each)
2 tbsp butter
2 cloves garlic, minced
1 cup heavy cream
1 cup grated Parmesan cheese
Salt and pepper

Directions

1. Cook pasta according to package instructions.
2. Season chicken with salt and pepper and cook in a pan until done.
3. In the same pan, melt butter and sauté garlic.
4. Stir in heavy cream and Parmesan cheese.
5. Serve over cooked pasta, topped with sliced chicken.

Fun Facts

Alfredo sauce is believed to have been created in Rome by restaurateur Alfredo di Lelio.

4 servings | 380 cal | 25 mins

Pesto Pasta with Grilled Chicken

A fresh and flavorful pasta dish with homemade basil pesto and tender grilled chicken.

Ingredients:

8 oz penne pasta
2 boneless, skinless chicken breasts (8 oz each)
For pesto: 2 cups fresh basil leaves
1/2 cup grated Parmesan cheese
1/4 cup pine nuts
2 cloves garlic
1/2 cup olive oil
Salt and pepper to taste

Directions

1. Cook pasta according to package instructions.
2. Season chicken with salt and pepper and grill until done.
3. In a food processor, blend basil, Parmesan, pine nuts, garlic, salt, and pepper.
4. With the motor running, drizzle in olive oil to make pesto.
5. Toss cooked pasta with pesto and top with sliced grilled chicken.

Fun Facts

Pesto is a sauce that originated in Genoa, Italy, and is known for its bright and fresh flavor.

4
servings

320 cal

20 mins

Greek Orzo Salad with Feta

A refreshing pasta salad with orzo, cherry tomatoes, cucumbers, olives, and crumbled feta cheese.

Ingredients:

1 cup orzo pasta
1 cup cherry tomatoes, halved
1/2 cup cucumber, diced
1/4 cup Kalamata olives, pitted and sliced
1/4 cup crumbled feta cheese
2 tbsp red wine vinegar
2 tbsp olive oil
Salt and pepper

Directions

1. Cook orzo according to package instructions and let it cool.
2. In a bowl, combine orzo, cherry tomatoes, cucumber, olives, and feta cheese.
3. Drizzle with red wine vinegar, olive oil, salt, and pepper.
4. Toss to combine. Serve chilled.

Fun Facts

Feta cheese is a staple in Greek cuisine, adding a creamy and tangy element to this salad.

4 servings | 360 cal | 25 mins

Shrimp Linguine with Garlic Butter

A delectable combination of tender shrimp and linguine pasta, all tossed in a luscious garlic butter sauce.

Ingredients:

8 oz linguine pasta
1 lb large shrimp, peeled and deveined
2 tbsp butter
4 cloves garlic, minced
1/4 cup fresh parsley, chopped
Juice of 1 lemon
Salt and pepper to taste

Directions

1. Cook pasta according to package instructions.
2. Season shrimp with salt and pepper and cook in a pan until pink.
3. In the same pan, melt butter and sauté garlic until fragrant.
4. Toss cooked pasta with shrimp, garlic butter, lemon juice, and parsley.
5. Serve hot.

Fun Facts

Garlic butter sauce is a classic and versatile element in pasta dishes, elevating their flavor.

4 servings | 410 cal | 20 mins

Spaghetti Carbonara

A Roman classic! Spaghetti carbonara is a rich pasta dish made with eggs, cheese, pancetta, and black pepper.

Ingredients:

8 oz spaghetti
1 cup pancetta or guanciale, diced
2 large eggs
1 cup grated Pecorino Romano cheese
1/4 cup grated Parmesan cheese
2 cloves garlic, minced
Black pepper to taste

Directions

1. Cook pasta according to package instructions.
2. In a skillet, sauté pancetta or guanciale until crispy.
3. In a bowl, whisk eggs, cheese, garlic, and black pepper.
4. Drain cooked pasta and toss with the egg mixture, adding pancetta. Serve hot.

Fun Facts

Carbonara has its roots in Italy and is loved for its rich and creamy sauce with a hint of smokiness.

4 servings | 380 cal | 30 mins

Beef and Mushroom Stroganoff

A hearty and creamy stroganoff with tender beef and sautéed mushrooms served over egg noodles.

Ingredients:

8 oz egg noodles
1 lb beef sirloin, thinly sliced
2 cups mushrooms, sliced
1 onion, chopped
2 cloves garlic, minced
1 cup beef broth
1/2 cup sour cream
2 tbsp Dijon mustard
2 tbsp flour
2 tbsp butter
Salt and pepper

Directions

1. Cook egg noodles according to package instructions.
2. In a skillet, brown beef slices and set aside.
3. In the same skillet, melt butter and sauté onions, garlic, and mushrooms until soft.
4. Stir in flour, Dijon mustard, and beef broth. Simmer until thickened.
5. Return beef to the skillet and add sour cream. Serve over cooked noodles.

Fun Facts

Stroganoff is a Russian dish originally made with beef, mushrooms, and sour cream.

4 servings

360 cal

25 mins

Blackened Salmon Pasta

A flavorful blackened salmon fillet served over pasta with a creamy lemon-dill sauce.

Ingredients:

8 oz penne pasta
4 salmon fillets (6 oz each)
2 tbsp blackened seasoning
2 tbsp olive oil
2 cloves garlic, minced
1 cup heavy cream
2 tbsp lemon juice
1 tsp dill, chopped
Salt and pepper to taste

Directions

1. Cook pasta according to package instructions.
2. Season salmon with blackened seasoning and cook in a pan with olive oil until done.
3. In the same pan, sauté garlic and stir in heavy cream, lemon juice, and dill.
4. Serve salmon over cooked pasta, topped with the creamy sauce.

Fun Facts

Blackened seasoning adds a smoky and spicy kick to the salmon, enhancing the overall flavor.

4 servings | 290 cal | 20 mins

Tuna Pasta Salad

Easy

A light and tangy pasta salad featuring flaked tuna, vegetables, and a zesty lemon vinaigrette.

Ingredients:

8 oz rotini pasta
2 cans (5 oz each) tuna, drained and flaked
1 cup cherry tomatoes, halved
1/2 cup red onion, finely chopped
1/4 cup black olives, sliced
2 tbsp olive oil
2 tbsp lemon juice
1 tsp Dijon mustard
Salt and pepper to taste

Directions

1. Cook pasta according to package instructions.
2. In a bowl, combine pasta, flaked tuna, cherry tomatoes, red onion, and olives.
3. Whisk together olive oil, lemon juice, Dijon mustard, salt, and pepper. Drizzle over the salad.

Fun Facts

Tuna is a great source of protein and adds a seafood twist to this pasta salad.

4 servings | 330 cal | 25 mins

Lemon Butter Shrimp Linguine

A delightful combination of shrimp and linguine with a zesty lemon-butter sauce, perfect for a quick dinner.

Ingredients:

8 oz linguine pasta
1 lb large shrimp, peeled and deveined
2 tbsp butter
4 cloves garlic, minced
Juice of 2 lemons
Zest of 1 lemon
1/4 cup fresh parsley, chopped
Salt and pepper to taste

Directions

1. Cook pasta according to package instructions.
2. Season shrimp with salt and pepper and cook in a pan until pink.
3. In the same pan, melt butter and sauté garlic until fragrant.
4. Stir in lemon juice, lemon zest, and parsley.
5. Toss cooked pasta with shrimp and lemon-butter sauce. Serve hot.

Fun Facts

Lemon adds a zesty and refreshing touch to this shrimp and pasta dish, brightening its flavor.

4 servings | 440 cal | 30 mins

Chicken and Broccoli Alfredo

A twist on classic Alfredo! Tender chicken and crisp broccoli florets served in a creamy Alfredo sauce.

Ingredients:

8 oz fettuccine pasta
2 boneless, skinless chicken breasts (8 oz each)
2 cups broccoli florets
2 tbsp butter
2 cloves garlic, minced
1 cup heavy cream
1 cup grated Parmesan cheese
Salt and pepper to taste

Directions

1. Cook pasta according to package instructions.
2. Season chicken with salt and pepper and cook in a pan until done.
3. In the same pan, melt butter and sauté garlic.
4. Stir in heavy cream and Parmesan cheese.
5. Add broccoli and simmer until tender.
6. Serve over cooked pasta, topped with sliced chicken.

Fun Facts

Alfredo sauce pairs wonderfully with broccoli, creating a rich and creamy combination.

We have a small favor to ask

Ladies and gentlemen, culinary aficionados, and fellow food enthusiasts,

I hope you're enjoying this flavorful journey through "5-Ingredient High-Protein Dishes." If you've already savored some of the dishes, you know that simplicity and protein-packed delights go hand in hand.

I want to take a moment to talk about something important – reviews. In the world of cookbooks and culinary adventures, reviews are like seasoning; they add an extra layer of flavor and depth. They help other aspiring chefs and gastronomes decide if this book is a culinary companion they'd like to invite into their kitchens.

Here's the honest truth – reviews can be elusive, like the perfect soufflé. As a small publishing team passionate about bringing you delicious recipes, reviews are hard to come by. That's where you, our cherished readers, come in.

If you've found these high-protein recipes to be a source of culinary inspiration, if one of the dishes has become your go-to meal, or if you simply appreciate the effort we put into crafting this cookbook, we kindly ask you for a small favor.

Please consider sharing your thoughts in a review. It doesn't need to be an essay; a few lines and a star rating can make all the difference. Your review is a gesture of support that can help others discover the joy of cooking with high-protein simplicity.

At the heart of it all, we're grateful that you've chosen "5-Ingredient High-Protein Dishes" for your culinary adventures. We read and appreciate every single review. Your feedback inspires us to keep creating recipes that cater to your culinary needs.

Now, let's get back to what truly matters – the recipes. The next dish is waiting to be discovered, and I'm excited to continue this delectable journey with you.

Thank you for your time and consideration.

Sincerely,

Garden of Grapes

Chapter 5: Bean and Legume Delights

4 servings | 220 cal | 20 mins

Three-Bean Salad

A colorful and nutritious salad featuring a trio of beans—green beans, kidney beans, and garbanzo beans.

Ingredients:

1 cup green beans, trimmed and cut
1 can (15 oz) kidney beans, drained
1 can (15 oz) garbanzo beans, drained
1/2 red onion, finely chopped
1/4 cup fresh parsley, chopped
2 tbsp olive oil
2 tbsp red wine vinegar
Salt and pepper to taste

Directions

1. Blanch green beans in boiling water for 2 mins, then cool.
2. In a large bowl, combine green beans, kidney beans, garbanzo beans, red onion, and parsley.
3. In a small bowl, whisk together olive oil, red wine vinegar, salt, and pepper.
4. Drizzle the dressing over the salad and toss to combine. Serve chilled.

Fun Facts

Three-bean salad is a classic side dish known for its blend of flavors and textures.

4 servings

360 cal

30 mins

Chili Con Carne

A hearty and spicy chili made with ground beef, beans, and a medley of spices, perfect for a cozy meal.

Ingredients:

1 lb ground beef
1 onion, chopped
2 cloves garlic, minced
1 can (15 oz) kidney beans, drained
1 can (15 oz) black beans, drained
1 can (15 oz) diced tomatoes
2 tbsp chili powder
1 tsp cumin
1 tsp paprika
Salt and pepper to taste

Directions

1. In a large pot, brown ground beef, onions, and garlic.
2. Add kidney beans, black beans, diced tomatoes, chili powder, cumin, paprika, salt, and pepper.
3. Simmer for 20 mins, stirring occasionally.
4. Serve hot with your choice of toppings.

Fun Facts

Chili con carne is a popular Tex-Mex dish, known for its bold and spicy flavors.

4 servings | 280 cal | 25 mins

Chickpea and Spinach Curry

A flavorful and vegetarian curry with chickpeas and spinach in a rich tomato-based sauce, served with rice.

Ingredients:

2 cans (15 oz each) chickpeas, drained
1 onion, chopped
2 cloves garlic, minced
1 can (14 oz) diced tomatoes
2 cups fresh spinach
2 tbsp curry powder
1 cup coconut milk
Salt and pepper to taste

Directions

1. In a pan, sauté onions and garlic until fragrant.
2. Add chickpeas, diced tomatoes, and curry powder.
3. Simmer for 15 mins.
4. Stir in spinach and coconut milk, and cook until spinach wilts.
5. Season with salt and pepper. Serve with rice.

Fun Facts

Chickpea and spinach curry is a popular Indian dish known for its aromatic spices and hearty ingredients.

4 servings

320 cal

25 mins

Black Bean Tacos

A vegetarian delight! These black bean tacos are filled with a savory mixture of black beans, veggies, and cheese.

Ingredients:

1 can (15 oz) black beans, drained
1 cup corn kernels
1 red bell pepper, diced
1/2 cup cheddar cheese, shredded
1/4 cup fresh cilantro, chopped
8 small flour tortillas
2 tbsp olive oil
2 tsp taco seasoning
Salt and pepper to taste

Directions

1. In a pan, heat olive oil and sauté red bell pepper until soft.
2. Add black beans, corn, taco seasoning, salt, and pepper, and cook for 5 mins.
3. Warm tortillas in a dry skillet.
4. Fill tortillas with the black bean mixture, top with cheese and cilantro. Serve hot.

Fun Facts

Black bean tacos are a popular Mexican dish, offering a flavorful and satisfying vegetarian option.

4 servings | 260 cal | 30 mins

Red Lentil Soup

A comforting and nourishing soup made with red lentils, vegetables, and a blend of spices.

Ingredients:

1 cup red lentils
1 onion, chopped
2 carrots, diced
2 cloves garlic, minced
1 tsp cumin
1 tsp paprika
6 cups vegetable broth
Salt and pepper to taste

Directions

1. In a pot, sauté onions, carrots, and garlic until soft.
2. Add red lentils, cumin, paprika, and vegetable broth.
3. Simmer for 20 mins until lentils are tender.
4. Season with salt and pepper. Serve hot.

Fun Facts

Red lentil soup is enjoyed in various cuisines worldwide and is known for its creamy and wholesome texture.

4
servings

380 cal

30 mins

White Bean and Sausage Stew

A hearty and flavorful stew featuring white beans, sausage, and a medley of vegetables in a rich tomato broth.

Ingredients:

1 lb Italian sausage, sliced
2 cans (15 oz each) white beans, drained
1 onion, chopped
2 cloves garlic, minced
1 can (14 oz) diced tomatoes
2 cups kale, chopped
4 cups chicken broth
2 tbsp olive oil
2 tsp Italian seasoning
Salt and pepper to taste

Directions

1. In a large pot, brown sausage slices in olive oil.
2. Add onions, garlic, Italian seasoning, and cook until onions are soft.
3. Stir in white beans, diced tomatoes, kale, and chicken broth.
4. Simmer for 15 mins. Season with salt and pepper. Serve hot.

Fun Facts

White bean and sausage stew offers a mix of savory and satisfying flavors, perfect for a comforting meal.

4 servings | 200 cal | 35 mins

Roasted Chickpeas

A crunchy and savory snack or topping made with roasted chickpeas and a blend of spices.

Ingredients:

2 cans (15 oz each) chickpeas, drained
2 tbsp olive oil
1 tsp cumin
1 tsp paprika
1/2 tsp cayenne pepper
Salt to taste

Directions

1. Preheat the oven to 400°F (200°C).
2. Toss chickpeas with olive oil, cumin, paprika, cayenne pepper, and salt.
3. Spread chickpeas on a baking sheet and roast for 25-30 mins, stirring occasionally.
4. Let them cool before serving.

Fun Facts

Roasted chickpeas are a crunchy and protein-packed snack, offering a satisfying alternative to chips.

4 servings

300 cal

30 mins

Lentil and Quinoa Bowl

A nutritious and satisfying bowl featuring lentils, quinoa, and a variety of colorful veggies.

Ingredients:

1 cup green or brown lentils
1/2 cup quinoa
2 cups vegetable broth
1 cup cherry tomatoes, halved
1 cup cucumber, diced
1/4 cup red onion, finely chopped
1/4 cup fresh parsley, chopped
2 tbsp lemon juice
2 tbsp olive oil
Salt and pepper to taste

Directions

1. Rinse lentils and quinoa.
2. In a pot, combine lentils, quinoa, vegetable broth, and bring to a boil. Simmer for 20 mins.
3. Let it cool.
4. In a bowl, combine cooked lentils and quinoa, cherry tomatoes, cucumber, red onion, and parsley.
5. Drizzle with lemon juice, olive oil, salt, and pepper. Serve chilled.

Fun Facts

Lentils and quinoa provide a satisfying and protein-rich base for this nutritious bowl.

4 servings

280 cal

20 mins

Bean and Avocado Salad

A refreshing and creamy salad featuring black beans, avocado, and a zesty lime dressing.

Ingredients:

2 cans (15 oz each) black beans, drained
2 avocados, diced
1/4 cup red onion, finely chopped
1/4 cup fresh cilantro, chopped
Juice of 2 limes
2 tbsp olive oil
Salt and pepper to taste

Directions

1. In a large bowl, combine black beans, diced avocados, red onion, and cilantro.
2. Drizzle with lime juice, olive oil, salt, and pepper. Toss to combine. Serve chilled.

Fun Facts

Black beans and avocados create a creamy and nutritious combination in this zesty salad.

4 servings | 260 cal | 35 mins

Split Pea Soup

A classic and comforting split pea soup made with green split peas, ham, and aromatic herbs.

Ingredients:

1 cup green split peas
1 onion, chopped
2 carrots, diced
1 ham hock or ham bone
4 cups chicken broth
2 bay leaves
1 tsp thyme
Salt and pepper to taste

Directions

1. In a pot, combine split peas, onions, carrots, ham hock, chicken broth, bay leaves, thyme, salt, and pepper.
2. Bring to a boil, then simmer for 25-30 mins until peas are tender.
3. Remove the ham hock or bone and bay leaves. Serve hot.

Fun Facts

Split pea soup is a classic comfort food, known for its rich and savory flavor.

Chapter 6: High-Protein Seafood Sensations

4 servings | 290 cal | 20 mins

Tuna Salad Stuffed Avocado

A light and refreshing dish featuring a savory tuna salad served in avocado halves.

Ingredients:

2 cans (5 oz each) canned tuna, drained
1/4 cup mayonnaise
1/4 cup Greek yogurt
1/2 red onion, finely chopped
1/2 celery stalk, finely chopped
1 tsp Dijon mustard
2 avocados
Juice of 1 lemon
Salt and pepper to taste

Directions

1. In a bowl, combine canned tuna, mayonnaise, Greek yogurt, red onion, celery, and Dijon mustard.
2. Cut avocados in half, remove the pits, and drizzle with lemon juice to prevent browning.
3. Fill avocado halves with tuna salad and season with salt and pepper. Serve chilled.

Fun Facts

Tuna salad stuffed avocados are a simple and elegant appetizer or light meal, packed with protein and healthy fats.

4 servings | 380 cal | 25 mins

Cajun Shrimp and Sausage Skillet

A spicy and flavorful skillet dish with shrimp and sausage, served over rice or pasta.

Ingredients:

1 lb large shrimp, peeled and deveined
8 oz andouille sausage, sliced
1 onion, chopped
1 red bell pepper, chopped
2 cloves garlic, minced
1 cup diced tomatoes
2 tsp Cajun seasoning
Cooked rice or pasta
Salt and pepper to taste

Directions

1. In a skillet, cook sausage until browned. Remove and set aside.
2. In the same skillet, sauté onions, garlic, and red bell pepper until soft.
3. Stir in shrimp, diced tomatoes, and Cajun seasoning. Cook until shrimp are pink.
4. Return sausage to the skillet, season with salt and pepper, and serve over cooked rice or pasta.

Fun Facts

Cajun seasoning adds a spicy and smoky kick to this shrimp and sausage dish, a popular Southern cuisine favorite.

4 servings | 320 cal | 25 mins

Lemon Herb Cod

A light and aromatic dish featuring cod fillets seasoned with zesty lemon and fresh herbs.

Ingredients:

4 cod fillets (6 oz each)
Juice of 2 lemons
2 cloves garlic, minced
2 tbsp fresh parsley, chopped
2 tbsp fresh dill, chopped
2 tbsp olive oil
Salt and pepper to taste

Directions

1. Preheat the oven to 375°F (190°C).
2. In a baking dish, arrange cod fillets.
3. Drizzle with lemon juice, olive oil, and sprinkle with garlic, parsley, dill, salt, and pepper.
4. Bake for 20 mins until cod flakes easily with a fork. Serve hot.

Fun Facts

Lemon and fresh herbs provide a bright and flavorful profile to this cod dish, enhancing its natural taste.

4 servings
340 cal
20 mins

Coconut Crusted Shrimp

A crispy and tropical delight! These shrimp are coated in coconut and served with a sweet chili dipping sauce.

Ingredients:

1 lb large shrimp, peeled and deveined
1 cup shredded coconut
1/2 cup panko breadcrumbs
2 eggs
1/4 cup all-purpose flour
1/4 cup sweet chili sauce
Salt and pepper to taste

Directions

1. Preheat the oven to 400°F (200°C).
2. In separate bowls, place flour, beaten eggs, and a mixture of shredded coconut and panko breadcrumbs.
3. Dredge each shrimp in flour, dip in eggs, and coat with coconut mixture.
4. Place on a baking sheet and bake for 10-12 mins until golden and crispy.
5. Serve with sweet chili sauce.

Fun Facts

Coconut-crusted shrimp provides a delightful tropical twist and a satisfying crunch to this seafood dish.

4 servings | 380 cal | 30 mins

Baked Salmon with Dill Sauce

A classic and elegant dish featuring baked salmon fillets served with a creamy dill sauce.

Ingredients:

4 salmon fillets (6 oz each)
Juice of 1 lemon
2 cloves garlic, minced
2 tbsp fresh dill, chopped
1/4 cup Greek yogurt
1/4 cup mayonnaise
2 tbsp Dijon mustard
Salt and pepper to taste

Directions

1. Preheat the oven to 375°F (190°C).
2. In a baking dish, arrange salmon fillets.
3. Drizzle with lemon juice and season with garlic, salt, and pepper.
4. Bake for 20 mins or until salmon flakes easily with a fork.
5. In a bowl, whisk together dill, Greek yogurt, mayonnaise, and Dijon mustard.
6. Serve salmon with dill sauce.

Fun Facts

Dill sauce complements salmon's natural flavors and adds a touch of creaminess to this classic dish.

4 servings | 330 cal | 25 mins

Teriyaki Tuna Steaks

A delicious fusion of flavors! These tuna steaks are marinated in a sweet and savory teriyaki sauce.

Ingredients:

4 tuna steaks (6 oz each)
1/2 cup teriyaki sauce
2 cloves garlic, minced
1/4 cup brown sugar
2 tbsp sesame oil
1 tsp ginger, grated
2 green onions, chopped
Cooked rice for serving
Salt and pepper to taste

Directions

1. In a bowl, combine teriyaki sauce, garlic, brown sugar, sesame oil, ginger, and green onions.
2. Marinate tuna steaks in the mixture for 15 mins.
3. Preheat a grill or skillet over medium-high heat.
4. Season tuna steaks with salt and pepper and grill for 2-3 mins per side, or to your desired doneness.
5. Serve over cooked rice.

Fun Facts

Teriyaki sauce offers a perfect balance of sweet and savory flavors, enhancing the taste of these tuna steaks.

4 servings | 320 cal | 20 mins

Garlic Lemon Butter Shrimp

A delightful combination of shrimp, garlic, lemon, and butter, served with pasta or crusty bread.

Ingredients:

1 lb large shrimp, peeled and deveined
4 cloves garlic, minced
Juice of 2 lemons
1/4 cup fresh parsley, chopped
4 tbsp butter
2 tbsp olive oil
Salt and pepper to taste

Directions

1. In a skillet, heat olive oil and 2 tbsp butter over medium heat.
2. Season shrimp with salt and pepper and cook for 2-3 mins per side until pink.
3. Remove shrimp from the skillet.
4. In the same skillet, melt the remaining 2 tbsp of butter and sauté garlic until fragrant.
5. Stir in lemon juice, parsley, and return the shrimp to the skillet.
6. Serve with pasta or crusty bread.

Fun Facts

Garlic lemon butter shrimp is a delightful combination of flavors, offering a zesty and buttery profile.

4 servings | 270 cal | 20 mins

Blackened Tilapia

A spicy and flavorful dish featuring tilapia fillets coated in blackening seasoning and seared to perfection.

Ingredients:

4 tilapia fillets (6 oz each)
2 tbsp blackening seasoning
2 tbsp olive oil
Juice of 1 lemon
Salt and pepper to taste

Directions

1. Preheat a skillet over medium-high heat.
2. Season tilapia fillets with salt, blackening seasoning, and pepper.
3. Drizzle with olive oil and place in the skillet.
4. Sear for 3-4 mins per side or until fish flakes easily with a fork.
5. Drizzle with lemon juice and serve hot.

Fun Facts

Blackening seasoning adds a spicy and smoky kick to the tilapia, creating a flavorful and satisfying seafood dish.

4 servings | 340 cal | 25 mins

Citrus Glazed Mahi-Mahi

A tangy and sweet dish featuring mahi-mahi fillets glazed with a zesty citrus sauce, perfect for a tropical meal.

Ingredients:

4 mahi-mahi fillets (6 oz each)
Juice of 2 oranges
Juice of 2 limes
1/4 cup honey
2 cloves garlic, minced
2 tbsp olive oil
1 tsp thyme
Salt and pepper to taste

Directions

1. In a bowl, combine orange juice, lime juice, honey, garlic, olive oil, thyme, salt, and pepper.
2. Marinate mahi-mahi fillets in the mixture for 15 mins.
3. Preheat a grill or skillet over medium-high heat.
4. Grill fish for 3-4 mins per side or until fish flakes easily with a fork.
5. Serve hot.

Fun Facts

Citrus glaze provides a zesty and refreshing element to this mahi-mahi dish, enhancing its tropical flavors.

4 servings | 300 cal | 20 mins

Mediterranean Tuna Salad

A Mediterranean-inspired tuna salad with olives, cucumbers, and feta cheese, served over a bed of greens.

Ingredients:

2 cans (5 oz each) canned tuna, drained
1/4 cup Kalamata olives, pitted and sliced
1/2 cup cucumber, diced
1/4 cup red onion, finely chopped
1/4 cup feta cheese, crumbled
Juice of 1 lemon
2 tbsp olive oil
1 tsp oregano
Salt and pepper to taste

Directions

1. In a bowl, combine canned tuna, olives, cucumber, red onion, and feta cheese.
2. Drizzle with lemon juice, olive oil, oregano, salt, and pepper.
3. Toss to combine.
4. Serve over a bed of greens.

Fun Facts

Mediterranean tuna salad offers a refreshing blend of flavors, combining the best of Mediterranean cuisine with canned tuna.

Chapter 7: Nutty and Seedy Creations

4 servings

360 cal

25 mins

Almond-Crusted Chicken

A crunchy and flavorful dish featuring chicken breasts coated in almond crust, perfect for a nutty twist.

Ingredients:

4 boneless, skinless chicken breasts (6 oz each)
1 cup almonds, finely chopped
1/2 cup grated Parmesan cheese
1/2 cup flour
2 eggs
1 tsp paprika
Salt and pepper to taste

Directions

1. Preheat the oven to 375°F (190°C).
2. In a bowl, combine finely chopped almonds, grated Parmesan, flour, and paprika.
3. In another bowl, beat the eggs.
4. Season chicken breasts with salt and pepper.
5. Dip each chicken breast in the beaten eggs, then coat with the almond mixture.
6. Place chicken on a baking sheet and bake for 20 mins or until golden and cooked through.

Fun Facts

Almond crust adds a satisfying crunch to this chicken dish, offering a delightful combination of textures.

4 servings | 320 cal | 20 mins

Walnut and Blue Cheese Salad

A salad filled with rich flavors! It combines walnuts, blue cheese, and a tangy vinaigrette for a nutty delight.

Ingredients:

4 cups mixed greens
1/2 cup walnuts, chopped
1/4 cup crumbled blue cheese
1/4 cup dried cranberries
2 tbsp balsamic vinaigrette
Salt and pepper to taste

Directions

1. In a large bowl, combine mixed greens, chopped walnuts, blue cheese, and dried cranberries.
2. Drizzle with balsamic vinaigrette and toss to coat.
3. Season with salt and pepper. Serve chilled.

Fun Facts

Walnuts and blue cheese create a rich and satisfying flavor profile in this salad, perfect for a quick and tasty meal.

4 servings | 280 cal | 25 mins

Cashew and Broccoli Stir-Fry

A quick and nutritious stir-fry featuring cashews, broccoli, and a savory sauce, served over rice or noodles.

Ingredients:

8 oz cashews
2 cups broccoli florets
1 lb chicken or tofu, cubed
2 cloves garlic, minced
2 tbsp soy sauce
1 tbsp oyster sauce
1 tbsp sesame oil
Cooked rice or noodles
Salt and pepper to taste

Directions

1. In a wok or large skillet, heat sesame oil over medium-high heat.
2. Add chicken or tofu and stir-fry until cooked through.
3. Stir in garlic, cashews, and broccoli, and cook for a few minutes.
4. Add soy sauce and oyster sauce, stirring well.
5. Season with salt and pepper.
6. Serve over cooked rice or noodles.

Fun Facts

Cashews and broccoli create a delightful combination of textures and flavors in this quick and easy stir-fry.

12 bites | 120 cal | 15 mins

Peanut Butter Energy Bites

A no-bake treat with the goodness of oats, peanut butter, honey, and chocolate chips, perfect for an energy boost.

Ingredients:

1 cup old-fashioned oats
1/2 cup peanut butter
1/3 cup honey
1/4 cup mini chocolate chips
1 tsp vanilla extract
Pinch of salt

Directions

1. In a bowl, combine oats, peanut butter, honey, chocolate chips, vanilla extract, and a pinch of salt.
2. Mix until well combined.
3. Roll the mixture into bite-sized balls.
4. Place in the fridge to firm up for about 30 mins.

Fun Facts

Peanut butter energy bites offer a quick and healthy snack option, providing a burst of energy with every bite.

4 servings | 320 cal | 20 mins

Sunflower Seed Chicken Salad

A vibrant salad featuring sunflower seeds, grilled chicken, and a tangy citrus dressing, perfect for a light meal.

Ingredients:

4 boneless, skinless chicken breasts (6 oz each)
1/4 cup sunflower seeds
4 cups mixed greens
1/2 cup cherry tomatoes, halved
1/4 cup red onion, finely chopped
Juice of 2 lemons
2 tbsp olive oil
1 tsp honey
Salt and pepper to taste

Directions

1. Preheat a grill or skillet over medium-high heat.
2. Season chicken breasts with salt and pepper and grill for 4-5 mins per side until cooked through.
3. In a large bowl, combine mixed greens, sunflower seeds, cherry tomatoes, and red onion.
4. In a separate bowl, whisk together lemon juice, olive oil, honey, salt, and pepper.
5. Slice grilled chicken and top the salad with it. Drizzle with the dressing. Serve chilled.

Fun Facts

Sunflower seeds add a delightful crunch to this chicken salad, while the citrus dressing provides a refreshing twist.

8 bars | 180 cal | 30 mins

Almond and Date Protein Bars

Homemade protein bars featuring almonds, dates, and a hint of honey, a nutritious and satisfying on-the-go snack.

Ingredients:

1 cup almonds
1 cup pitted dates
1/4 cup honey
1/4 cup almond butter
1/4 cup unsweetened cocoa powder
1 tsp vanilla extract
Pinch of salt

Directions

1. In a food processor, blend almonds, dates, honey, almond butter, cocoa powder, vanilla extract, and a pinch of salt until a dough forms.
2. Press the mixture into a lined baking pan and refrigerate for 20-30 mins until firm.
3. Cut into bars and enjoy.

Fun Facts

These almond and date protein bars are a healthy and convenient snack option, perfect for satisfying your hunger.

4 servings | 330 cal | 25 mins

Normal

Pumpkin Seed Crusted Salmon

A unique and flavorful salmon dish featuring a pumpkin seed crust and a zesty cilantro-lime dressing.

Ingredients:

4 salmon fillets (6 oz each)
1/2 cup pumpkin seeds
2 cloves garlic, minced
1/4 cup fresh cilantro, chopped
Juice of 2 limes
2 tbsp olive oil
Salt and pepper to taste

Directions

1. Preheat the oven to 375°F (190°C).
2. In a food processor, blend pumpkin seeds, garlic, cilantro, lime juice, olive oil, salt, and pepper until a coarse paste forms.
3. Season salmon fillets with salt and pepper.
4. Spread the pumpkin seed mixture over the salmon.
5. Bake for 15-20 mins or until salmon flakes easily with a fork. Serve with extra dressing.

Fun Facts

Pumpkin seed crust adds a unique and nutty flavor to this salmon dish, while the cilantro-lime dressing provides a zesty kick.

4 servings

340 cal

30 mins

Sesame Chicken

A classic and flavorful dish featuring crispy chicken pieces coated in sesame seeds and a savory sauce.

Ingredients:

1 lb boneless, skinless chicken breasts, cut into pieces
1/4 cup flour
2 eggs
1/2 cup sesame seeds
2 tbsp soy sauce
1 tbsp honey
2 cloves garlic, minced
1 tsp ginger, grated
Cooked rice for serving
Salt and pepper to taste

Directions

1. In one bowl, place flour. In another bowl, beat eggs. In a third bowl, spread sesame seeds.
2. Season chicken pieces with salt and pepper.
3. Dip chicken pieces in flour, then eggs, and coat with sesame seeds.
4. In a skillet, heat oil over medium-high heat and fry chicken pieces until golden and cooked through.
5. In a separate bowl, combine soy sauce, honey, garlic, and ginger.
6. Serve sesame chicken over cooked rice, drizzled with the sauce.

Fun Facts

Sesame seeds add a delightful crunch to this classic chicken dish, while the savory sauce enhances its flavor.

4 servings

360 cal

25 mins

Pecan-Crusted Pork Chops

A nutty twist on pork chops! These are coated in pecans and served with a sweet and tangy apple chutney.

Ingredients:

4 pork chops (6 oz each)
1 cup pecans, finely chopped
1/4 cup bread crumbs
2 eggs
1 tsp paprika
1/2 cup applesauce
1/4 cup apple cider vinegar
2 tbsp brown sugar
Salt and pepper to taste

Directions

1. Preheat the oven to 375°F (190°C).
2. Season pork chops with salt, pepper, and paprika.
3. In one bowl, place finely chopped pecans and bread crumbs.
4. In another bowl, beat eggs.
5. Dip pork chops in the beaten eggs, then coat with the pecan mixture.
6. Place on a baking sheet and bake for 20 mins or until pork is cooked through.
7. In a saucepan, combine applesauce, apple cider vinegar, brown sugar, and cook until thickened.
8. Serve pork chops with apple chutney.

Fun Facts

Pecan crust provides a rich and nutty flavor to these pork chops, while the apple chutney adds a sweet and tangy contrast.

4 servings

280 cal

20 mins

Easy

Quinoa Salad with Almonds

A nutritious and satisfying salad featuring quinoa, almonds, and a zesty lemon vinaigrette.

Ingredients:

1 cup quinoa
1/2 cup almonds, chopped
1/2 cup cucumber, diced
1/4 cup red onion, finely chopped
1/4 cup fresh parsley, chopped
Juice of 2 lemons
2 tbsp olive oil
Salt and pepper to taste

Directions

1. Rinse quinoa and cook according to package instructions.
2. In a bowl, combine cooked quinoa, chopped almonds, cucumber, red onion, and fresh parsley.
3. In a separate bowl, whisk together lemon juice, olive oil, salt, and pepper.
4. Drizzle the vinaigrette over the salad and toss to combine. Serve chilled.

Fun Facts

Quinoa and almonds create a nutritious and flavorful base for this salad, while the lemon vinaigrette adds a zesty kick.

Chapter 8: Protein-Rich Dairy Delights

2 servings | 230 cal | 10 mins

Greek Yogurt Parfait

A simple and wholesome treat featuring Greek yogurt, granola, and fresh berries, perfect for breakfast or dessert.

Ingredients:

2 cups Greek yogurt
1 cup granola
1 cup mixed berries (e.g., strawberries, blueberries, raspberries)
2 tbsp honey

Directions

1. In two glasses or bowls, layer Greek yogurt, granola, and mixed berries.
2. Drizzle with honey.
3. Repeat the layers.
4. Serve chilled.

Fun Facts

Greek yogurt parfaits are a nutritious and delightful way to start your day or satisfy your sweet cravings.

2 servings | 220 cal | 10 mins

Cottage Cheese and Pineapple

A refreshing and creamy snack featuring cottage cheese and pineapple chunks, a perfect balance of sweet and savory.

Ingredients:

2 cups cottage cheese
1 cup pineapple chunks (fresh or canned, drained)
1 tbsp honey
Mint leaves for garnish

Directions

1. In two bowls, divide the cottage cheese and pineapple chunks.
2. Drizzle with honey.
3. Garnish with mint leaves.
4. Serve chilled.

Fun Facts

Cottage cheese and pineapple offer a harmonious blend of flavors and textures, making it a satisfying and healthy snack.

4 servings | 290 cal | 30 mins

Ricotta Stuffed Peppers

A savory dish featuring bell peppers stuffed with a rich and creamy ricotta cheese filling, baked to perfection.

Ingredients:

4 bell peppers (any color)
1 cup ricotta cheese
1/4 cup grated Parmesan cheese
1/4 cup fresh basil, chopped
2 cloves garlic, minced
1/2 cup marinara sauce
Salt and pepper to taste

Directions

1. Preheat the oven to 375°F (190°C).
2. Cut the tops off the bell peppers and remove the seeds and membranes.
3. In a bowl, combine ricotta cheese, grated Parmesan, basil, garlic, salt, and pepper.
4. Stuff each bell pepper with the ricotta mixture.
5. Place the peppers in a baking dish, pour marinara sauce over them.
6. Cover with foil and bake for 20-25 mins, then uncover and bake for an additional 10 mins until peppers are tender and the filling is golden.
7. Serve hot.

Fun Facts

Ricotta-stuffed peppers offer a creamy and savory combination, perfect for a satisfying and wholesome meal.

4 servings | 260 cal | 20 mins

Cottage Cheese Pancakes

Fluffy and protein-packed pancakes made with cottage cheese, a delicious breakfast or brunch option.

Ingredients:

1 cup cottage cheese
1/2 cup flour
2 eggs
1 tbsp sugar
1/2 tsp baking powder
1/4 tsp salt
1/4 cup milk
2 tbsp butter
Maple syrup or jam for serving

Directions

1. In a blender, combine cottage cheese, flour, eggs, sugar, baking powder, salt, and milk. Blend until smooth.
2. Heat a skillet or griddle over medium heat and melt a little butter.
3. Pour pancake batter onto the skillet to form pancakes of your desired size.
4. Cook until bubbles form on the surface, then flip and cook the other side until golden.
5. Serve hot with maple syrup or jam.

Fun Facts

Cottage cheese pancakes are a fluffy and protein-rich alternative to traditional pancakes, making a hearty breakfast.

2 servings | 180 cal | 5 mins

Yogurt and Berry Smoothie

A creamy and fruity smoothie featuring yogurt and a medley of mixed berries, a refreshing and nutritious drink.

Ingredients:

2 cups Greek yogurt
1 cup mixed berries (e.g., strawberries, blueberries, raspberries)
1/2 cup milk
2 tbsp honey
Ice cubes (optional)

Directions

1. In a blender, combine Greek yogurt, mixed berries, milk, honey, and ice cubes if desired.
2. Blend until smooth and creamy.
3. Pour into glasses and serve chilled.

Fun Facts

Yogurt and berry smoothies offer a refreshing and nutritious way to enjoy the goodness of dairy and fruits in one drink.

2 servings | 280 cal | 10 mins

Mascarpone and Berries

A luscious dessert featuring mascarpone cheese and a medley of fresh berries, perfect for a sweet and creamy treat.

Ingredients:

1 cup mascarpone cheese
1 cup mixed berries (e.g., strawberries, blueberries, raspberries)
2 tbsp honey
Mint leaves for garnish

Directions

1. In two bowls, divide the mascarpone cheese and mixed berries.
2. Drizzle with honey.
3. Garnish with mint leaves.
4. Serve chilled.

Fun Facts

Mascarpone and berries create a rich and creamy dessert, offering a delightful combination of flavors and textures.

4 servings | 230 cal | 15 mins

Cottage Cheese and Tomato Salad

A light and savory salad featuring cottage cheese, ripe tomatoes, and a zesty vinaigrette, a perfect side or snack.

Ingredients:

2 cups cottage cheese
2 cups cherry tomatoes, halved
1/4 cup fresh basil, chopped
2 tbsp olive oil
1 tbsp balsamic vinegar
Salt and pepper to taste

Directions

1. In a large bowl, combine cottage cheese, cherry tomatoes, and fresh basil.
2. In a separate bowl, whisk together olive oil, balsamic vinegar, salt, and pepper.
3. Drizzle the vinaigrette over the salad and toss to combine.
4. Serve chilled.

Fun Facts

Cottage cheese and tomato salad provides a light and refreshing option, featuring the best of fresh ingredients and dairy.

4 servings | 320 cal | 35 mins

Ricotta and Spinach Stuffed Chicken Breast

A hearty dish featuring chicken breasts stuffed with a creamy ricotta and spinach filling, a gourmet meal at home.

Ingredients:

4 boneless, skinless chicken breasts (6 oz each)
1 cup ricotta cheese
1 cup chopped spinach
1/4 cup grated Parmesan cheese
2 cloves garlic, minced
1/2 cup marinara sauce
Salt and pepper to taste

Directions

1. Preheat the oven to 375°F (190°C).
2. In a bowl, combine ricotta cheese, chopped spinach, grated Parmesan, garlic, salt, and pepper.
3. Cut a slit into each chicken breast to create a pocket.
4. Stuff each chicken breast with the ricotta mixture.
5. Place the stuffed chicken breasts in a baking dish, pour marinara sauce over them.
6. Cover with foil and bake for 25 mins, then uncover and bake for an additional 10 mins until chicken is cooked through.
7. Serve hot.

Fun Facts

Ricotta and spinach-stuffed chicken breasts offer a gourmet dining experience at home, with a rich and creamy filling.

4 servings | 290 cal | 30 mins

Greek Yogurt Chicken

A tender and tangy chicken dish featuring Greek yogurt, lemon, and herbs, perfect for a flavorful and protein-rich meal.

Ingredients:

4 boneless, skinless chicken breasts (6 oz each)
1 cup Greek yogurt
Juice of 2 lemons
2 cloves garlic, minced
1 tsp dried oregano
1 tsp dried thyme
Salt and pepper to taste

Directions

1. Preheat the oven to 375°F (190°C).
2. Season chicken breasts with salt, pepper, dried oregano, and dried thyme.
3. In a bowl, combine Greek yogurt, lemon juice, and minced garlic.
4. Spread the yogurt mixture over the chicken breasts.
5. Place in a baking dish and bake for 25-30 mins or until chicken is cooked through and yogurt is golden.
6. Serve hot.

Fun Facts

Greek yogurt chicken offers a tender and tangy flavor profile, with the yogurt keeping the chicken moist and flavorful.

4 servings | 350 cal | 40 mins

Ricotta and Spinach Stuffed Shells

A comforting pasta dish featuring jumbo pasta shells filled with a creamy ricotta and spinach mixture, baked with marinara sauce and cheese.

Ingredients:

20 jumbo pasta shells
2 cups ricotta cheese
1 cup chopped spinach
1/4 cup grated Parmesan cheese
2 cloves garlic, minced
1/2 cup mozzarella cheese, shredded
1/2 cup marinara sauce
Salt and pepper to taste

Directions

1. Preheat the oven to 375°F (190°C).
2. Cook pasta shells according to package instructions, then drain and set aside.
3. In a bowl, combine ricotta cheese, chopped spinach, grated Parmesan, garlic, salt, and pepper.
4. Stuff each cooked pasta shell with the ricotta mixture.
5. Spread marinara sauce in the bottom of a baking dish.
6. Place the stuffed shells in the dish, top with mozzarella cheese.
7. Cover with foil and bake for 20 mins, then uncover and bake for an additional 10 mins until the cheese is bubbly and golden.
8. Serve hot.

Fun Facts

Ricotta and spinach-stuffed shells offer a comforting and cheesy pasta dish, perfect for a satisfying family dinner.

Chapter 9: Protein-Packed Salad Bowls

4 servings | 320 cal | 30 mins

Grilled Chicken Caesar Salad

A classic salad featuring grilled chicken, crisp romaine lettuce, croutons, and Caesar dressing, a satisfying meal.

Ingredients:

4 boneless, skinless chicken breasts (6 oz each)
2 heads romaine lettuce, chopped
1 cup croutons
1/2 cup grated Parmesan cheese
1/4 cup Caesar dressing
Salt and pepper to taste

Directions

1. Preheat the grill to medium-high heat.
2. Season chicken breasts with salt and pepper.
3. Grill chicken for 6-8 mins per side or until cooked through.
4. Slice grilled chicken.
5. In a large bowl, combine chopped romaine, croutons, and grated Parmesan cheese.
6. Add grilled chicken slices.
7. Drizzle with Caesar dressing and toss to coat.
8. Serve immediately.

Fun Facts

Grilled chicken Caesar salad is a satisfying and flavorful classic, offering a perfect balance of textures and tastes.

4 servings | 290 cal | 25 mins

Quinoa and Chickpea Salad

A nutritious and protein-packed salad featuring quinoa, chickpeas, and a medley of vegetables, a hearty and tasty dish.

Ingredients:

1 cup quinoa
1 can (15 oz) chickpeas, drained and rinsed
1 cup cucumber, diced
1 cup cherry tomatoes, halved
1/4 cup red onion, finely chopped
Juice of 2 lemons
2 tbsp olive oil
1/4 cup fresh parsley, chopped
Salt and pepper to taste

Directions

1. Rinse quinoa and cook according to package instructions.
2. In a large bowl, combine cooked quinoa, chickpeas, diced cucumber, cherry tomatoes, and red onion.
3. Drizzle with lemon juice and olive oil.
4. Add chopped fresh parsley and toss to combine.
5. Season with salt and pepper.
6. Serve chilled.

Fun Facts

Quinoa and chickpea salad offers a protein-packed and nutrient-rich option, perfect for a hearty and wholesome meal.

4 servings | 380 cal | 35 mins

Steak and Avocado Salad

A hearty salad featuring seared steak, creamy avocado, mixed greens, and a zesty vinaigrette, a satisfying and robust meal.

Ingredients:

1 lb sirloin steak
2 avocados, sliced
8 cups mixed greens
1/4 cup red onion, finely chopped
2 tbsp balsamic vinaigrette
2 tbsp olive oil
Salt and pepper to taste

Directions

1. Preheat a grill or skillet over high heat.
2. Season steak with salt and pepper.
3. Sear the steak for 3-4 mins per side or to your desired doneness.
4. Let the steak rest for a few minutes, then slice it.
5. In a large bowl, combine mixed greens, sliced avocado, and finely chopped red onion.
6. In a separate bowl, whisk together balsamic vinaigrette, olive oil, salt, and pepper.
7. Drizzle the vinaigrette over the salad and toss to coat.
8. Top with sliced steak.
9. Serve immediately.

Fun Facts

Steak and avocado salad offers a hearty and robust flavor profile, with the creamy avocado complementing the seared steak.

4 servings | 350 cal | 30 mins

Tuna Nicoise Salad

A French classic salad featuring seared tuna, boiled eggs, potatoes, green beans, and olives, a delightful and complete meal.

Ingredients:

4 tuna steaks (6 oz each)
4 eggs
2 cups small potatoes, boiled and halved
2 cups green beans, blanched
1 cup cherry tomatoes, halved
1/2 cup Kalamata olives, pitted
2 tbsp Dijon dressing
Salt and pepper to taste

Directions

1. Season tuna steaks with salt and pepper.
2. Preheat a grill or skillet over high heat.
3. Sear tuna steaks for 2-3 mins per side or to your desired doneness.
4. Let the tuna rest and slice.
5. In a saucepan, boil eggs, then peel and halve them.
6. In a large bowl, combine boiled potatoes, blanched green beans, cherry tomatoes, pitted olives, and sliced boiled eggs.
7. Drizzle with Dijon dressing and toss to coat.
8. Top with sliced tuna steaks.
9. Serve warm or at room temperature.

Fun Facts

Tuna Nicoise salad is a complete and delightful meal, offering a range of flavors and textures in one dish.

4 servings

290 cal

25 mins

Spinach and Chicken Salad

A refreshing salad featuring grilled chicken, fresh spinach, strawberries, and a balsamic vinaigrette, a delightful and light meal.

Ingredients:

4 boneless, skinless chicken breasts (6 oz each)
8 cups fresh spinach
2 cups strawberries, sliced
1/4 cup red onion, finely chopped
2 tbsp balsamic vinaigrette
2 tbsp olive oil
Salt and pepper to taste

Directions

1. Preheat the grill to medium-high heat.
2. Season chicken breasts with salt and pepper.
3. Grill chicken for 6-8 mins per side or until cooked through.
4. Slice grilled chicken.
5. In a large bowl, combine fresh spinach, sliced strawberries, and finely chopped red onion.
6. In a separate bowl, whisk together balsamic vinaigrette, olive oil, salt, and pepper.
7. Drizzle the vinaigrette over the salad and toss to coat.
8. Top with sliced chicken.
9. Serve immediately.

Fun Facts

Spinach and chicken salad offers a refreshing and light combination of ingredients, with the sweetness of strawberries.

4 servings | 270 cal | 20 mins

Black Bean and Corn Salad

A zesty and colorful salad featuring black beans, sweet corn, bell peppers, and a lime-cilantro dressing, a flavorful and hearty dish.

Ingredients:

2 cans (15 oz each) black beans, drained and rinsed
2 cups sweet corn (fresh or frozen)
1 cup red bell pepper, diced
1 cup green bell pepper, diced
1/2 cup red onion, finely chopped
Juice of 2 limes
1/4 cup fresh cilantro, chopped
2 tbsp olive oil
Salt and pepper to taste

Directions

1. In a large bowl, combine black beans, sweet corn, diced red and green bell peppers, and finely chopped red onion.
2. Drizzle with lime juice and olive oil.
3. Add chopped fresh cilantro and toss to combine.
4. Season with salt and pepper.
5. Serve chilled.

Fun Facts

Black bean and corn salad offers a zesty and colorful medley of flavors, with a hint of lime and cilantro for freshness.

4 servings | 340 cal | 30 mins

Salmon and Quinoa Bowl

A protein-packed bowl featuring grilled salmon, quinoa, roasted vegetables, and a lemon-tahini dressing, a nutritious and filling meal.

Ingredients:

4 salmon fillets (6 oz each)
1 cup quinoa
2 cups mixed vegetables (e.g., bell peppers, zucchini, carrots)
2 tbsp olive oil
Juice of 2 lemons
2 tbsp tahini
Salt and pepper to taste

Directions

1. Preheat the grill to medium-high heat.
2. Season salmon fillets with salt and pepper.
3. Grill salmon for 4-5 mins per side or until cooked through.
4. In a saucepan, rinse quinoa and cook according to package instructions.
5. Toss mixed vegetables with olive oil, salt, and pepper, then roast in the oven at 400°F (200°C) for 15-20 mins or until tender.
6. In a bowl, whisk together lemon juice, tahini, salt, and pepper.
7. In serving bowls, divide cooked quinoa, roasted vegetables, and grilled salmon.
8. Drizzle with lemon-tahini dressing.
9. Serve warm.

Fun Facts

Salmon and quinoa bowl is a nutritious and filling meal, offering a variety of textures and a burst of flavors.

4 servings | 320 cal | 30 mins

Normal

Turkey and Cranberry Salad

A Thanksgiving-inspired salad featuring roasted turkey, cranberries, mixed greens, and a cranberry vinaigrette, a delightful and festive dish.

Ingredients:

4 cups roasted turkey, shredded
2 cups mixed greens
1 cup dried cranberries
1/2 cup pecans, chopped
1/4 cup red onion, finely chopped
2 tbsp cranberry vinaigrette
Salt and pepper to taste

Directions

1. In a large bowl, combine roasted turkey, mixed greens, dried cranberries, chopped pecans, and finely chopped red onion.
2. Drizzle with cranberry vinaigrette and toss to coat.
3. Season with salt and pepper.
4. Serve chilled.

Fun Facts

Turkey and cranberry salad offers a delightful and festive twist on a classic salad, perfect for celebrating Thanksgiving all year round.

4 servings | 310 cal | 25 mins

Greek Chicken Salad

A Mediterranean-inspired salad featuring grilled chicken, cucumbers, tomatoes, olives, and feta cheese, a flavorful and vibrant meal.

Ingredients:

4 boneless, skinless chicken breasts (6 oz each)
2 cucumbers, diced
2 cups cherry tomatoes, halved
1/2 cup Kalamata olives, pitted
1/2 cup feta cheese, crumbled
2 tbsp Greek dressing
Salt and pepper to taste

Directions

1. Preheat the grill to medium-high heat.
2. Season chicken breasts with salt and pepper.
3. Grill chicken for 6-8 mins per side or until cooked through.
4. Slice grilled chicken.
5. In a large bowl, combine diced cucumbers, halved cherry tomatoes, pitted olives, and crumbled feta cheese.
6. Drizzle with Greek dressing and toss to coat.
7. Top with sliced chicken.
8. Serve immediately.

Fun Facts

Greek chicken salad offers a flavorful and vibrant combination of Mediterranean ingredients, with a tangy Greek dressing.

4 servings | 260 cal | 20 mins

Edamame and Sesame Salad

A Japanese-inspired salad featuring edamame, mixed greens, sesame seeds, and a ginger-soy dressing, a light and exotic dish.

Ingredients:

2 cups shelled edamame
8 cups mixed greens
1/4 cup sesame seeds
2 tbsp ginger-soy dressing
Salt and pepper to taste

Directions

1. Steam edamame according to package instructions, then let them cool.
2. In a large bowl, combine steamed edamame, mixed greens, and sesame seeds.
3. Drizzle with ginger-soy dressing and toss to coat.
4. Season with salt and pepper.
5. Serve chilled.

Fun Facts

Edamame and sesame salad offers a light and exotic flavor profile, with the nuttiness of sesame seeds and the zing of ginger-soy dressing.

Chapter 10: Savory High-Protein Sides

4 servings | 180 cal | 20 mins

Garlic Butter Green Beans with Almonds

A flavorful side dish featuring sautéed green beans in garlic butter, garnished with toasted almonds, a simple yet delicious addition.

Ingredients:

1 lb green beans, trimmed
2 tbsp butter
3 cloves garlic, minced
1/4 cup slivered almonds
Juice of 1 lemon
Salt and pepper to taste

Directions

1. In a large skillet, melt butter over medium heat.
2. Add minced garlic and sauté for 1-2 mins until fragrant.
3. Add green beans, season with salt and pepper, and sauté for 8-10 mins until tender-crisp.
4. In a separate pan, toast slivered almonds until lightly browned.
5. Drizzle lemon juice over the green beans.
6. Sprinkle toasted almonds on top.
7. Serve hot.

Fun Facts

Garlic butter green beans with almonds offer a simple yet flavorful side dish that complements various main courses.

4 servings | 220 cal | 30 mins

Parmesan and Garlic Roasted Brussels Sprouts

A crispy and cheesy side featuring roasted Brussels sprouts with garlic and Parmesan, a delightful and savory addition.

Ingredients:

1 lb Brussels sprouts, trimmed and halved
2 tbsp olive oil
3 cloves garlic, minced
1/2 cup grated Parmesan cheese
Salt and pepper to taste

Directions

1. Preheat the oven to 400°F (200°C).
2. In a large bowl, toss Brussels sprouts with olive oil, minced garlic, salt, and pepper.
3. Spread them on a baking sheet in a single layer.
4. Roast for 20-25 mins until crispy and browned.
5. Sprinkle grated Parmesan cheese over the roasted sprouts.
6. Return to the oven for an additional 5 mins until the cheese is melted and bubbly.
7. Serve hot.

Fun Facts

Parmesan and garlic roasted Brussels sprouts offer a crispy and savory side, perfect for cheese lovers.

4 servings | 280 cal | 25 mins

Quinoa Pilaf

A wholesome and protein-rich side featuring quinoa cooked with aromatic herbs, vegetables, and toasted nuts, a complete and flavorful accompaniment.

Ingredients:

1 cup quinoa
2 cups vegetable broth
1/2 cup chopped onions
1/2 cup chopped bell peppers (any color)
1/2 cup chopped carrots
1/4 cup chopped celery
1/4 cup slivered almonds
2 tbsp olive oil
1 tsp dried thyme
1 tsp dried oregano
Salt and pepper to taste

Directions

1. In a saucepan, heat olive oil over medium heat.
2. Sauté chopped onions, bell peppers, carrots, and celery until softened.
3. Add quinoa and cook for 2-3 mins, stirring frequently.
4. Stir in dried thyme, dried oregano, salt, and pepper.
5. Pour in vegetable broth and bring to a boil.
6. Reduce heat, cover, and simmer for 15 mins or until quinoa is cooked and liquid is absorbed.
7. In a separate pan, toast slivered almonds until golden.
8. Fluff the quinoa with a fork, then sprinkle toasted almonds on top.
9. Serve hot.

Fun Facts

Quinoa pilaf is a complete and flavorful side dish, offering a nutritious blend of quinoa, vegetables, and aromatic herbs.

4 servings | 200 cal | 25 mins

Buffalo Cauliflower Bites

Easy

A spicy and addictive side featuring roasted cauliflower florets coated in Buffalo sauce, a bold and fiery addition.

Ingredients:

1 head cauliflower, cut into florets
1/2 cup hot sauce (e.g., Frank's RedHot)
2 tbsp melted butter
1 tsp garlic powder
1 tsp paprika
1/2 tsp cayenne pepper (adjust to taste)
Ranch or blue cheese dressing for dipping (optional)
Salt and pepper to taste

Directions

1. Preheat the oven to 450°F (230°C).
2. In a large bowl, combine hot sauce, melted butter, garlic powder, paprika, cayenne pepper, salt, and pepper.
3. Toss cauliflower florets in the Buffalo sauce until well coated.
4. Spread them on a baking sheet in a single layer.
5. Roast for 20-25 mins until crispy and browned.
6. Serve hot with ranch or blue cheese dressing for dipping if desired.

Fun Facts

Buffalo cauliflower bites are a bold and fiery side that adds a spicy kick to your meal.

4 servings | 240 cal | 20 mins

Protein-Packed Coleslaw

Easy

A nutritious and protein-rich coleslaw featuring shredded cabbage, carrots, Greek yogurt, and sunflower seeds, a creamy and wholesome side.

Ingredients:

4 cups shredded cabbage
1 cup shredded carrots
1 cup Greek yogurt
2 tbsp mayonnaise
1 tbsp Dijon mustard
2 tbsp apple cider vinegar
2 tbsp honey
1/4 cup sunflower seeds
Salt and pepper to taste

Directions

1. In a large bowl, combine shredded cabbage and carrots.
2. In a separate bowl, whisk together Greek yogurt, mayonnaise, Dijon mustard, apple cider vinegar, honey, salt, and pepper.
3. Pour the creamy dressing over the coleslaw and toss to coat.
4. Sprinkle sunflower seeds on top.
5. Serve chilled.

Fun Facts

Protein-packed coleslaw is a creamy and wholesome side that provides extra nutrition and a delightful crunch.

4 servings | 160 cal | 15 mins

Grilled Asparagus with Feta

Easy

A simple and elegant side featuring grilled asparagus spears, crumbled feta cheese, and a drizzle of balsamic reduction, a delightful and gourmet addition.

Ingredients:

1 lb asparagus spears, trimmed
2 tbsp olive oil
1/2 cup crumbled feta cheese
Balsamic reduction (store-bought or homemade)
Salt and pepper to taste

Directions

1. Preheat the grill to medium-high heat.
2. Toss asparagus spears with olive oil, salt, and pepper.
3. Grill asparagus for 4-6 mins, turning occasionally, until tender and lightly charred.
4. Arrange grilled asparagus on a serving platter.
5. Sprinkle crumbled feta cheese over the asparagus.
6. Drizzle with balsamic reduction.
7. Serve hot or at room temperature.

Fun Facts

Grilled asparagus with feta offers a simple yet elegant side with the perfect balance of flavors.

4 servings | 210 cal | 30 mins

Normal

Mediterranean Stuffed Mushrooms

A flavorful side featuring mushroom caps stuffed with a Mediterranean-inspired mixture of spinach, feta, and herbs, a gourmet and savory addition.

Ingredients:

16 large mushroom caps
2 cups chopped spinach
1/2 cup crumbled feta cheese
2 cloves garlic, minced
1/4 cup fresh parsley, chopped
2 tbsp olive oil
Salt and pepper to taste

Directions

1. Preheat the oven to 375°F (190°C).
2. Remove stems from mushroom caps and set aside.
3. In a skillet, heat olive oil over medium heat.
4. Sauté minced garlic and chopped spinach until wilted.
5. Remove from heat and stir in crumbled feta, fresh parsley, salt, and pepper.
6. Fill each mushroom cap with the spinach-feta mixture.
7. Place stuffed mushrooms on a baking sheet.
8. Bake for 20 mins or until mushrooms are tender and filling is golden.
9. Serve hot.

Fun Facts

Mediterranean stuffed mushrooms offer a gourmet and savory side dish that's perfect for entertaining.

4 servings | 240 cal | 25 mins

Easy

Cilantro Lime Rice

A zesty side featuring fluffy rice cooked with fresh cilantro, lime juice, and a hint of garlic, a vibrant and aromatic addition.

Ingredients:

2 cups long-grain white rice
4 cups water
1 cup fresh cilantro leaves
Juice of 2 limes
2 cloves garlic, minced
Salt to taste

Directions

1. Rinse rice in cold water until the water runs clear.
2. In a saucepan, bring 4 cups of water to a boil.
3. Add rice and cook until tender, then drain and set aside.
4. In a blender, combine fresh cilantro, lime juice, minced garlic, and salt.
5. Blend until smooth.
6. Fluff the cooked rice with a fork and drizzle the cilantro-lime mixture over it.
7. Toss to coat.
8. Serve warm.

Fun Facts

Cilantro lime rice offers a vibrant and aromatic side that pairs well with a variety of main dishes.

4 servings | 160 cal | 20 mins

Balsamic Glazed Carrots

A sweet and tangy side featuring glazed baby carrots cooked with balsamic vinegar and honey, a delightful and colorful addition.

Ingredients:

1 lb baby carrots
2 tbsp balsamic vinegar
2 tbsp honey
2 tbsp butter
Salt and pepper to taste

Directions

1. In a skillet, melt butter over medium heat.
2. Add baby carrots and sauté for 5 mins until slightly tender.
3. Stir in balsamic vinegar, honey, salt, and pepper.
4. Continue to cook for 10 mins until the carrots are glazed and tender.
5. Serve hot.

Fun Facts

Balsamic glazed carrots offer a delightful and colorful side with a perfect balance of sweet and tangy flavors.

4 servings

220 cal

30 mins

Spiced Chickpea Fries

A crispy and flavorful side featuring chickpea fries coated in a blend of spices, a unique and addictive addition.

Ingredients:

2 cans (15 oz each) chickpeas, drained and rinsed
2 tbsp olive oil
1 tsp paprika
1 tsp cumin
1/2 tsp cayenne pepper (adjust to taste)
1/2 tsp garlic powder
Salt and pepper to taste

Directions

1. Preheat the oven to 425°F (220°C).
2. Pat dry chickpeas with a clean kitchen towel to remove excess moisture.
3. In a bowl, toss chickpeas with olive oil, paprika, cumin, cayenne pepper, garlic powder, salt, and pepper.
4. Spread seasoned chickpeas on a baking sheet in a single layer.
5. Roast for 25-30 mins until chickpeas are crispy and browned.
6. Serve hot.

Fun Facts

Spiced chickpea fries offer a unique and addictive side with a satisfying crunch and a blend of aromatic spices.

Chapter 11: Sweet and Protein-Powered Desserts

2 servings | 240 cal | 10 mins

Protein-Packed Chocolate Smoothie

A creamy and indulgent chocolate smoothie packed with protein, a guilt-free treat that satisfies your sweet tooth.

Ingredients:

2 cups unsweetened almond milk
2 scoops chocolate protein powder
2 tbsp unsweetened cocoa powder
1 banana
1 tbsp almond butter
1 tsp honey
1/2 tsp vanilla extract
Ice cubes (optional)

Directions

1. In a blender, combine almond milk, chocolate protein powder, cocoa powder, banana, almond butter, honey, and vanilla extract.
2. Add ice cubes if desired for a thicker texture.
3. Blend until smooth and creamy.
4. Pour into glasses and enjoy.

Fun Facts

A protein-packed chocolate smoothie is a guilt-free indulgence that provides a delicious way to boost your protein intake.

12 balls | 100 cal | 20 mins

Peanut Butter Protein Balls

Nutty and satisfying protein balls made with peanut butter, oats, and honey, a portable and energizing snack.

Ingredients:

1 cup rolled oats
1/2 cup peanut butter
1/4 cup honey
1/4 cup protein powder (vanilla or chocolate)
1/4 cup chopped nuts (e.g., almonds, walnuts)
1/4 cup chocolate chips (optional)

Directions

1. In a large bowl, combine rolled oats, peanut butter, honey, protein powder, chopped nuts, and chocolate chips if using.
2. Mix until well combined.
3. Form the mixture into small balls and place them on a baking sheet lined with parchment paper.
4. Refrigerate for about 10-15 mins until the balls firm up.
5. Store in an airtight container.

Fun Facts

Peanut butter protein balls are a convenient and energizing snack that's perfect for on-the-go enjoyment.

2 servings

180 cal

15 mins

Greek Yogurt and Berry Parfait

A layered dessert featuring Greek yogurt, fresh berries, and a drizzle of honey, a healthy and refreshing treat.

Ingredients:

1 cup Greek yogurt
1 cup mixed berries (e.g., strawberries, blueberries, raspberries)
2 tbsp honey
1/4 cup granola (optional)
Fresh mint leaves for garnish (optional)

Directions

1. In two serving glasses or bowls, add a layer of Greek yogurt.
2. Top with a layer of mixed berries.
3. Drizzle honey over the berries.
4. Repeat the layers as desired.
5. Optionally, sprinkle granola on top for added crunch.
6. Garnish with fresh mint leaves if desired.
7. Serve immediately.

Fun Facts

Greek yogurt and berry parfait offers a healthy and refreshing dessert that's both satisfying and vibrant.

4 servings | 280 cal | 25 mins

Chocolate Protein Pancakes

Fluffy and chocolatey protein pancakes made with whey protein, a delectable and guilt-free breakfast or dessert.

Ingredients:

1 cup all-purpose flour
2 scoops chocolate whey protein powder
2 tbsp unsweetened cocoa powder
2 tbsp sugar
2 tsp baking powder
1/2 tsp salt
1 cup milk
1 egg
2 tbsp vegetable oil
1 tsp vanilla extract

Directions

1. In a large bowl, whisk together all-purpose flour, chocolate whey protein powder, cocoa powder, sugar, baking powder, and salt.
2. In a separate bowl, combine milk, egg, vegetable oil, and vanilla extract.
3. Pour the wet ingredients into the dry ingredients and stir until just combined.
4. Heat a non-stick skillet or griddle over medium heat and grease with cooking spray or butter.
5. Pour 1/4 cup of the pancake batter onto the skillet for each pancake.
6. Cook until bubbles form on the surface, then flip and cook the other side until golden.
7. Serve with your favorite toppings, such as fresh berries or maple syrup.

Fun Facts

Chocolate protein pancakes are a delectable and guilt-free way to enjoy the flavors of chocolate for breakfast or dessert.

8 bars

220 cal

30 mins

Almond and Protein Bars

Homemade protein bars with almonds, oats, and protein powder, a wholesome and satisfying snack for any time of day.

Ingredients:

1 cup rolled oats
1/2 cup chopped almonds
2 scoops vanilla protein powder
1/4 cup honey
1/4 cup almond butter
1/4 cup dried cranberries (optional)
1/4 cup dark chocolate chips (optional)

Directions

1. In a large bowl, combine rolled oats, chopped almonds, protein powder, honey, almond butter, dried cranberries, and dark chocolate chips if using.
2. Mix until well combined.
3. Press the mixture into a square or rectangular dish lined with parchment paper.
4. Refrigerate for about 20-25 mins until the bars firm up.
5. Cut into bars and store in an airtight container.

Fun Facts

Almond and protein bars are a wholesome and satisfying snack that can be customized with your favorite add-ins.

4 servings | 200 cal | 30 mins

Super Easy

Vanilla Protein Ice Cream

A creamy and protein-packed ice cream made with vanilla protein powder, a guilt-free and indulgent dessert.

Ingredients:

2 cups frozen banana slices
2 scoops vanilla protein powder
1/2 cup unsweetened almond milk
1 tsp vanilla extract
Honey or maple syrup for added sweetness (optional)

Directions

1. In a blender, combine frozen banana slices, vanilla protein powder, almond milk, and vanilla extract.
2. Blend until smooth and creamy.
3. Taste and add honey or maple syrup if you desire additional sweetness.
4. Transfer the mixture to an airtight container and freeze for 20-30 mins or until the ice cream is firm.
5. Scoop and serve.

Fun Facts

Vanilla protein ice cream is a guilt-free and creamy dessert that's perfect for those seeking a protein boost.

8 slices | 190 cal | 45 mins

Protein-Packed Banana Bread

A moist and flavorful banana bread with added protein from whey powder, a delightful and nutritious baked treat.

Ingredients:

3 ripe bananas
2 cups all-purpose flour
2 scoops vanilla whey protein powder
1/2 cup sugar
1/4 cup vegetable oil
1/4 cup Greek yogurt
1 tsp vanilla extract
1 tsp baking powder
1/2 tsp baking soda
1/2 tsp salt
1/2 tsp cinnamon
1/4 tsp nutmeg
2 eggs

Fun Facts

Protein-packed banana bread is a delightful and nutritious baked treat that combines the goodness of bananas and protein.

Directions

1. Preheat the oven to 350°F (175°C) and grease a loaf pan.
2. In a large bowl, mash the ripe bananas.
3. Add flour, vanilla whey protein powder, sugar, vegetable oil, Greek yogurt, vanilla extract, baking powder, baking soda, salt, cinnamon, nutmeg, and eggs to the mashed bananas.
4. Mix until well combined.
5. Pour the batter into the greased loaf pan.
6. Bake for 45 mins to 1 hour, or until a toothpick inserted into the center comes out clean.
7. Allow the banana bread to cool before slicing and serving.

4 servings | 160 cal | 20 mins

Easy

Chocolate Protein Mousse

A luscious and chocolatey protein mousse made with Greek yogurt and protein powder, a guilt-free and decadent dessert.

Ingredients:

1 cup Greek yogurt
2 scoops chocolate protein powder
2 tbsp unsweetened cocoa powder
2 tbsp honey
1/2 tsp vanilla extract
Chocolate shavings or cocoa powder for garnish (optional)

Directions

1. In a bowl, whisk together Greek yogurt, chocolate protein powder, cocoa powder, honey, and vanilla extract.
2. Mix until smooth and creamy.
3. Taste and adjust the sweetness if needed.
4. Spoon the mousse into serving glasses or bowls.
5. Garnish with chocolate shavings or a dusting of cocoa powder if desired.
6. Chill in the refrigerator for at least 15-20 mins before serving.
7. Enjoy your guilt-free chocolate protein mousse.

Fun Facts

Chocolate protein mousse is a guilt-free and decadent dessert that satisfies your chocolate cravings with added protein.

12 cookies | 130 cal | 25 mins

Peanut Butter Protein Cookies

Chewy and protein-packed peanut butter cookies made with protein powder and honey, a satisfying and guilt-free sweet treat.

Ingredients:

1 cup peanut butter
1/2 cup protein powder (vanilla or chocolate)
1/4 cup honey
1 egg
1/2 tsp vanilla extract
1/4 tsp salt

Directions

1. Preheat the oven to 350°F (175°C) and line a baking sheet with parchment paper.
2. In a bowl, combine peanut butter, protein powder, honey, egg, vanilla extract, and salt.
3. Mix until the dough comes together.
4. Drop spoonfuls of cookie dough onto the prepared baking sheet.
5. Flatten each cookie slightly with a fork to create a crisscross pattern.
6. Bake for 10-12 mins or until the edges are golden.
7. Allow the cookies to cool on the baking sheet for a few minutes before transferring to a wire rack to cool completely.
8. Enjoy your chewy peanut butter protein cookies.

Fun Facts

Peanut butter protein cookies are a satisfying and guilt-free sweet treat for peanut butter enthusiasts.

12 bites | 180 cal | 35 mins

Protein-Rich Cheesecake Bites

Mini cheesecake bites made with protein powder, Greek yogurt, and a graham cracker crust, a creamy and protein-rich dessert.

Ingredients:

For the crust:
1 cup graham cracker crumbs
3 tbsp melted butter
For the filling:
2 cups cream cheese, softened
1/2 cup Greek yogurt
2 scoops vanilla protein powder
1/2 cup sugar
2 eggs
1 tsp vanilla extract

Fun Facts

Protein-rich cheesecake bites are a creamy and protein-packed dessert with the classic flavors of cheesecake.

Directions

For the crust:
1. Preheat the oven to 350°F (175°C) and line a muffin tin with paper liners.
2. In a bowl, combine graham cracker crumbs and melted butter.
3. Divide the mixture evenly among the paper liners and press down to create the crust.
4. Bake for 5 mins and remove from the oven.

For the filling:
1. In a large bowl, beat cream cheese until smooth.
2. Add Greek yogurt, vanilla protein powder, sugar, eggs, and vanilla extract.
3. Mix until well combined.
4. Pour the filling over the graham cracker crust in each liner.
5. Bake for 20-25 mins or until the edges are set but the centers are slightly jiggly.
6. Allow the cheesecake bites to cool in the muffin tin, then refrigerate for at least 2 hours before serving.
7. Enjoy your protein-rich cheesecake bites.

We have a small favor to ask

Dear Food Enthusiasts,

As you savor the last morsels of your culinary journey through "5-Ingredient High-Protein Dishes," we want to express our heartfelt gratitude for choosing our cookbook to be your culinary companion. Your kitchen, much like the world of cuisine, is an exciting adventure, and we are thrilled to have been a part of it.

In the realm of cookbooks and culinary literature, our book is a small fish in a big sea. Yet, it's the readers, like you, who add the spices and flavors to our creations and bring them to life. Reviews are the treasures we food-loving explorers seek, and they are often as rare as a perfectly seared steak.

This is why we're reaching out to you, our fellow gastronomes, to kindly ask for your feedback. If our cookbook has graced your kitchen with delectable high-protein creations, we'd be immensely honored if you could take a moment to share your thoughts in a review.

We understand the value of your time, and we recognize that life is busy and filled with an abundance of choices. However, your review, whether a few lines or a brief sentence, can be the guiding star for others seeking culinary inspiration.

For us, a small team of passionate food enthusiasts, your reviews are like seasoning to our dishes. They not only add depth and flavor to our work but also provide us with the motivation to continue crafting recipes that resonate with you.

We're aware that, despite our best efforts, even the most seasoned chefs can make an occasional mistake. Rest assured, we are committed to learning from our errors and perfecting our recipes for future editions.

As we bid adieu to "5-Ingredient High-Protein Dishes," we want to extend our gratitude for your trust, your time, and the shared love of food. Your presence in this culinary journey has made it extraordinary, and we appreciate you being a part of it.

If you could find a moment in your culinary calendar, please consider revisiting the platform where you discovered this cookbook and sharing your experiences. A star rating, a sentence, or a few lines about your culinary adventures with our recipes would mean the world to us.

May your kitchen continue to be a haven of high-protein delights, and may your culinary path be paved with delicious discoveries. From our kitchen to yours, we wish you an endless array of delectable high-protein creations.

With sincere appreciation,

Garden of Grapes